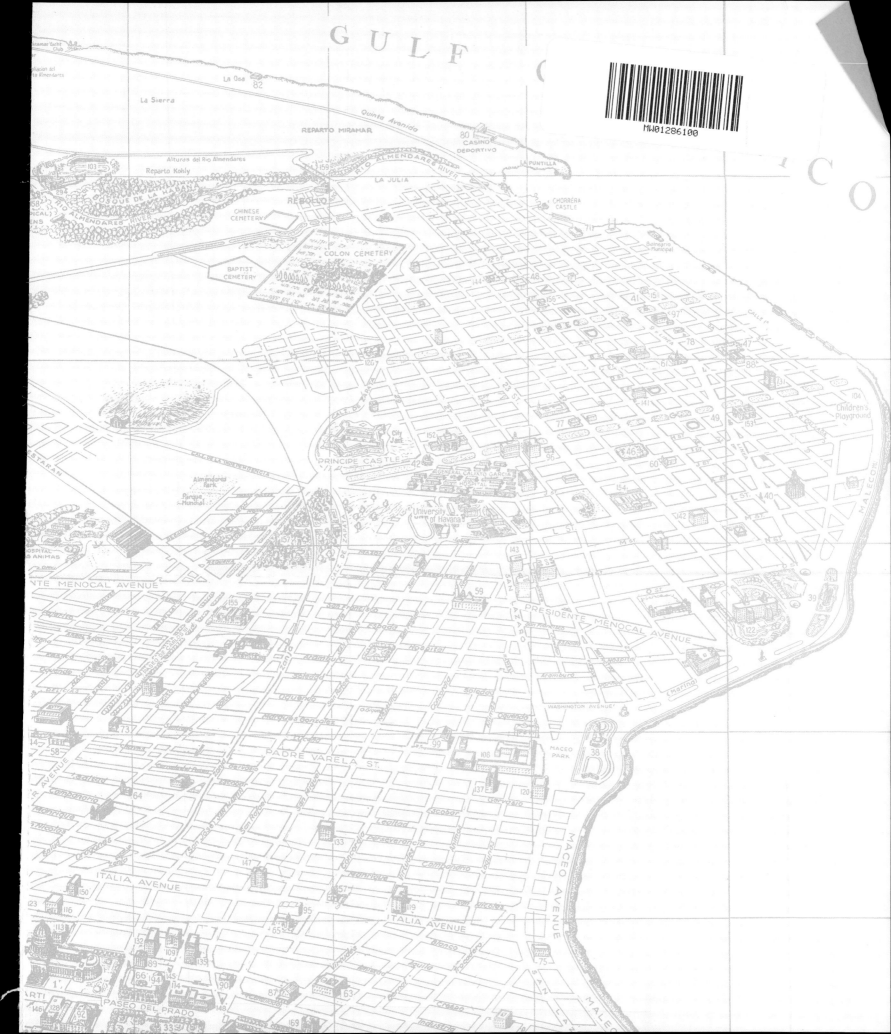

HAVANA MODERN

HAVANA MODERN

20th-Century Architecture and Interiors

MICHAEL CONNORS

Foreword by Ricardo Porro
Principle photography by Néstor Martí

ENDPAPERS 1947 Havana panoramic street map by Ramiro E. Iglesias, commissioned by the Cuban Tourist Commission.

PAGE 2 Detail of the FOCSA apartment building (Fomento de Obras y Construcciones, S.A.) in Havana's Vedado neighborhood, completed in 1956.

PAGES 4/5 View from one of Havana's Riviera Hotel balconies overlooking the Straits of Florida. Havana was considered the "Riviera of the Caribbean" in 1957 when the hotel opened. The building's curved design is reminiscent of an ocean wave and its color was meant to match the Caribbean Sea.

PAGES 6/7 View from the lobby balcony of the 1941 América Theatre.

PAGES 8/9 Passageway to the sea beneath thin-shell concrete vaults at the Club Náutico, a beach club in Havana's Playa district, designed by Max Borges Jr. in 1953.

PAGES 10/11 Entrance to one of Havana's monuments to modernism: Hospital de Maternidad Obrera (Workers' Maternity Hospital), which opened in 1940.

CONTENTS

Dedication — 15

Foreword — 18

Introduction — 22

Havana Modern — 82

Acknowledgments — 254

Endnotes — 255

ABOVE A 1965 aerial view of Ricardo Porro's National School of Fine Arts. This image displays the symbolic representation of figurative iconography that would later prove to be controversial.

OVERLEAF Ricardo Porro's National School of Modern Dance, built in 1965.

PAGE 19 Aerial view of Porro's National School of Modern Dance. Porro planned to represent metaphorically a sheet of glass that had been smashed and fragmented to symbolize the 1959 revolution's overthrow of the old order.

PAGES 20/21 A second-floor room overlooking the gallery and courtyard in the Palacio de los Capitanes Generales. Originally this palace was the Spanish governor's residence and the official seat of government for the colonial rulers until 1898. This style of old-world living ended by the close of the nineteenth century: "*Es anticuado vivir en la ciudad*" (Living in the city is old-fashioned). During the republic it was the Presidencial palace until 1920 and the City Hall until 1959. Since 1967 it has been the Havana City Museum.

DEDICATION

During the past several years of researching and writing in Cuba, I concluded that Cuban architects of the modernist movement have historically never been fully evaluated and that their contributions to architecture deserved further study and documentation. These beliefs led me to seek out world-renowned Cuban-born architect Ricardo Porro, who studied at the School of Architecture in Havana in the 1940s and practiced his art during the city's modernist years of the late 1940s, 1950s, and early 1960s. It is Porro, most famous for being the lead architect of Havana's enormously ambitious National Schools of Art, who is the spirit and source of inspiration for *Havana Modern: 20th-Century Architecture and Interiors*.

As part of the research for my previous book, *The Splendor of Cuba: 450 Years of Architecture and Interiors* (2011), I met Ricardo Porro and his wife, Elena, a multilingual interpreter, a few years ago in Paris. Over the course of our lengthy discussions about his childhood and life in Cuba, his beliefs and writings on twentieth-century architecture, art, the nature of beauty, and the role of the artist, I became convinced that my next book project would feature Havana's mid-twentieth-century modernist movement. Porro gave meaning to a mid-century Cuban architectural tradition that did not exist at that time. His architecture was imbued with meaningful symbolic content, often with erotic and anthropomorphic references, that continued to be a distinctive and constant characteristic of his work in Havana. Much of the symbolism derived from the Afro-Cuban beliefs that are an important part of Porro's discourse on the search for an indigenous expression of *Cubanidad* (that which is Cuban) resonates in his architecture.

Porro moved from Havana to Paris in 1966; there he continues to practice architecture and create art. France has awarded him the titles Chevalier de la Légion d'honneur and Commandeur de l'ordre des Arts et des Lettres, and in Italy, in 2012, he received the Premio Vittorio De Sica for architecture for his work on the National Schools of Art in Havana.

Porro's beliefs and teachings about architecture can be studied through two of his books: *Oeuvres/Obras: 1950–1993* and *Les cinq aspects du contenu* (both 1993). In both works Porro's quintessential *Cubanidad* is evident, and I asked him to share a few of these observations and thoughts with my readers in the foreword that follows.

FOREWORD

Ricardo Porro

I am an architect, a painter, a sculptor, and a poet. Here I will speak as an architect.

An architect is a technician. Woe to him if he isn't! His projects will probably be rejected. If they're accepted, woe to those who live in them! A building must be functional, well built, and built to last. And then there is that small matter of money: he must work within a budget. (Architects whose work is poor in spirit often use this constraint as an excuse.)

Yes, indeed, architecture is difficult. As an architect, I'm an artist, and how could it be otherwise? Creating a frame for the life of others is an architect's craft, and his art. Before beginning a project he must be familiar with the activities it will house, for he must conceive an architecture that respects, facilitates, and dignifies the life of those who will live in it. Although abstract architecture has prevailed for some time, I'm not an abstract architect; my work is figurative and meaningful. With very few exceptions meaning has been banished from architecture. I define architecture as the creation of a poetic frame for human activity. Architecture is also the transmutation of the world into living spaces. Every work of art is form and content. Form in my architecture isn't classic, it is closer to baroque. It's dynamic; a rhythm accompanies those who move around it.

Space is unlimited, as in baroque architecture. I've often said that a building should accompany the life of those who use it, but that is not enough. We should also be aware that it modifies its urban environment. The spaces on the outside should favor contact between those who use them.

I consider myself a romantic architect; I identify with Novalis [Georg Philipp Friedrich Freiherr von Hardenberg (1772–1801)] when he says, "Giving an elevated meaning to what is common, a mysterious aspect to the banal, the dignity of the unknown to what is known, a halo of infinity to the finite, I romanticize." I want my architecture to be rooted in the cultural environment where it belongs. That I did in Cuba, the country where I was born.

The Industrial Revolution that began in the nineteenth century reached its full development in the twentieth century and saw the triumph of technology. We find it reflected in Fernand Léger's painting and in Le Corbusier [Charles Édouard Jeanneret], when he speaks of the house as "a machine for living."

I conceived Havana's National Schools of Art during the first romantic phase of the Cuban revolution, when everything still seemed possible. I was in love with the revolution, and maybe it was this emotional impact that triggered a new conception in my architecture, the result of a dialogue between the world in which I lived and my own work. For the first time I conceived a building following a method I had gradually developed in my search for the meaning of architecture.

My intention was to create an architecture reflecting both the Spanish and African-Cuban cultural traditions, and my reader may legitimately ask how much of all this has been transmitted to those who see my work. The author of a work can give no answer, because each person will have his own view. Furthermore, someone may see something the author expressed unintentionally.

French literary critic Charles Augustin Sainte-Beuve wrote, "The greatest poet is not he who has done the best, it is he who suggests the most; he, not all of whose meaning is at first obvious, and who leaves you much to desire, to explain, to study, much to complete in your turn."

INTRODUCTION

The development of modern architecture in Cuba occurred during the first half of the twentieth century, and it was during those years that Cuba accomplished its most unprecedented achievements in both civic and domestic architecture. What is most surprising is that even though Havana has examples of every Western architectural style that exists from the past five hundred years (and many of the Western Hemisphere's most important monuments from previous centuries), the largest part of Cuba's capital city was built in the sixty years from independence in 1902 to the mid-twentieth-century revolution in 1959.

Four centuries of Spanish colonial rule ended after Cuba's third uprising against the crown since 1868, the War of Independence (1895–1898); during the last three months the United States intervened in the struggle in what became known as the Spanish-American War, snatching victory from the Cubans. The actual birth of Cuban independence was delayed for another four years (1898–1902) by the first of two U.S. military occupations of the island. Once the Cuban flag was raised in Havana on May 20, 1902, a Cuban republic was born and faced the challenging task of forging a new national cultural identity, one based on a more modern civil society. Cuba's three rebellions for independence lasted from 1868 to 1898 and financially exhausted what was considered in the nineteenth century to be a relatively vibrant island economy. The wars also virtually paralyzed any large-scale construction for decades.

By the close of the nineteenth century a small degree of modernity had been established in Cuba, particularly in Havana. Basic infrastructural elements, including railways, fresh water, electricity, limited telephone service, and automobiles, were available. Select Havana hotels had installed Cuba's first elevators and refurbished interiors with bathrooms that had built-in showers. During the late nineteenth century and into the early twentieth Cuba's modernization slowly progressed, but just as the old *criollo* (Creole) aristocracy continued to linger in faded grandeur, the island's architectural styles were characterized by both an unconscious continuation of traditionalism and a conscious dependence on designs of the immediate past.

Although Havana's School of Arts and Sciences (Facultad de Letras y Ciencias) added curricula in civil engineering, electrical engineering, and architecture in 1900, the advent of the twentieth century did not bring immediate or radical changes in architecture or interior design; rather, there was a transitional period that clung to late nineteenth-century styles, which included neoclassicism, neocolonialism, and a peninsular Beaux-Arts eclecticism. Derived from the academic teaching of the world center for architectural education, the École des Beaux-Arts in Paris, Beaux-Arts architecture typically embraced the styles of antiquity, the Renaissance, and seventeenth- and eighteenth-century France.

Eventually the spread of technology, industrialism, and a desire for the latest in domestic conveniences, together with political, economic, and social changes, launched a new phase of modernity in Havana's architecture. European and American tastes and ideas embodied the highest aspirations of the twentieth-century modern era and started to infiltrate and influence Cuban architectural education. It also began to liberate Cuban architecture students from the bondage of École des Beaux-Arts teachings. Over time Beaux-Arts style became less popular and the theories of functionalism,

PREVIOUS Sitting room in one of the many upper-class Havana homes built during the first decades of the twentieth century.

LEFT Exterior of a Vedado house built in the Beaux-Arts style popular in the early 1920s and still occupied by one of the original owners. After the 1959 revolution, the Cuban government seized commercial assets but not residences of the people who elected to stay on the island. A few members of the upper class remained and were able to keep their homes.

RIGHT View from the entrance hall to the dining room of the Vedado Beaux-Arts home.

LEFT Library of the Vedado Beaux-Arts house with the original furnishings. Built by Alonso Solís, who lived there with his wife, Blanca Soler, his son, José Miguel, and his daughter-in-law, Jossie Alonso. Jossie continues to live in the house.

RIGHT Bathroom stained-glass window and original tile work.

ABOVE Much of the mahogany furniture in early twentieth-century Havana homes was manufactured in Cuba.

RIGHT The majority of early twentieth-century Beaux-Arts homes in Havana are deteriorating because of lack of maintenance, but many have been preserved and appreciated.

ABOVE This dining room has managed to remain intact for the last ninety years.

in which form follows function, emerged, spawning a demand for more modernity in domestic as well as civic architecture.

During these same early years, Cuba's newly gained independence was aligned with an influx of foreign investment never before experienced in the island's history. Concurrent with the influx of investments came waves of immigrants, a phenomenon also unparalleled in its history. Cuba's capital city, Havana, expanded more rapidly than at any other time in its four-hundred-year existence. As the historian Hugh Thomas points out, "Between 1902 and 1910 almost 200,000 Spaniards, mostly Gallegos [Galicians] or Asturians emigrated to Cuba . . . Spanish emigration in these years was ironically higher than at any time when she herself owned the colonies."[1]

Among the half a million immigrants who arrived in Cuba during the first quarter of the twentieth century were architects, artisans, builders, and sculptors who had been trained and who had cultivated their trades, talents, and tastes under the mantle of the European moderne movement.

During the second U.S. military occupation, from 1906 to 1909, Cuba once again found itself under foreign control. (American marines returned in 1912 to quell racial disturbances and again in 1917 to control unrest among political factions.) During these years Havana continued to be a grand, imposing city and to see radical architectural changes. By this time the antique baroque marble palaces of the nobles in the old city had begun to be vacated, and, as historian Thomas explains, "in their place came new fashions: under the occupation there had been much silly imitation of North American practices, leading to light, wood, hot houses without an internal courtyard, most unsuitable for hurricanes; then there had been under Estrada [Cuba's first president, General Tomás Estrada

ABOVE The staircase and second-floor landing railings show the intricate ironwork that Cuban artisans were capable of in the early twentieth century.

Palma, 1902–6] and even under Magoon [Charles E. Magoon, provisional U.S. governor during the second American occupancy] a 'Catalan phase,' inspired by Spanish immigrants themselves influenced by the contemporary flourishing of art nouveau, Gaudí, and many fantasies beloved by the Barcelona bourgeoisie."[2]

Soon the newest fashion in design, specifically the art nouveau style, arrived from Europe and flourished especially in Havana, with Catalan, Viennese, Belgian, and French versions in overlapping successions. The term "art nouveau," coined in France, described a movement in the art world and referred to La Maison de l'Art Nouveau, an art gallery founded in Paris in 1895 by the German dealer Siegfried Bing.

Art nouveau, known as *modernismo* in Spanish and *modernista* in Catalan, is considered a key element in the beginning of the modern movement in Cuba insofar as it rejected the previous decades' classical historicism and eclectic revival styles of the island's architecture and decorative fashions. Art nouveau's popular ornamental and decorative motifs were based on nature and the sensuous, swooping organic curvilinear forms of flowers and plants. The style informed design in masonry, carpentry, stained glass, metalwork, and furniture. In addition, and more importantly, Havana's art nouveau movement led to the art deco style and eventually to modernism in Cuban architecture.

The appearance of the Cuban magazine *Arquitectura* in 1917 signaled a formal reassessment of the past four hundred years of Cuban architecture and aesthetics. Stimulated by both continuing Spanish and American immigration and additional foreign investment, businesses, banks, construction and trading companies multiplied rapidly, and the buildings erected to house them became an essential manifestation of not only Cuba's new republic, but

PREVIOUS The Palacio del Centro Asturiano (Palace of the Asturian Center) was designed by Spanish architect Manuel del Busto and built for the Asturian Society, a club that served members of Cuba's aristocratic class native to the northwestern Spanish Province of Asturias. It opened in 1927 and today houses the Museo de Bellas Artes (Fine Arts Museum), which is dedicated to Cuba's European art collection.

LEFT The grand staircase of the Palacio del Centro Asturiano is one of the most spectacular in all of Cuba and conforms to the purist classicism of the Spanish Renaissance style.

ABOVE The leaded stained-glass dome above the staircase depicts Christopher Columbus's three ships discovering the New World.

ABOVE A blend of Spanish and Italian Renaissance Revival influenced the Beaux-Arts façade of Havana's Estación Terminal de Trenes (Central Railway Station), designed by American architect Kenneth McKenzie Murchison and built in 1912. The bell towers have elevators, staircases, and bathrooms.

RIGHT The Spanish and Italian Renaissance Revival–inspired style of Lonja del Comercio (Commercial Exchange Building) on the Plaza de San Francisco was in keeping with the Beaux-Arts fashion of the day. Designed by Spanish architect Tomás Mur and built by the American engineering firm of Purdy & Henderson, it was completed in 1909 and originally included a bank, stores, and offices.

also the definitive changes in architectural style and interior design taste. Rises in sugar prices on the world markets during World War I (partially due to the destruction of the sugar beet industry in Europe at the time) led to further wealth that brought about a fresh era of constructing costly mansions, *palacios*, and civic buildings. In addition, there was a renewal of interest in various professional schools, such as the Colegio de Arquitectos de La Habana (Havana's School of Architecture), which created new curricula and opportunities for exchanging ideas and, more importantly, marked the beginning of a collective rejection of past Spanish colonial architecture in favor of new international trends.

Cuba's early to mid-twentieth-century modern architecture movement can be seen as having two major phases. The first began a few years before World War I and continued to World War II. While it paid homage to Beaux-Arts influences with eclectic Cuban interruptions, it also formulated and developed new design ideas that were expressions of the ever-increasing interest in American engineering techniques and architectural trends. The second phase lasted from World War II to the mid-1960s and, under the impact of rectilinear cubism, emphasized the theories of modernist architects such as, notably, Ludwig Mies van der Rohe, Frank Lloyd Wright, Walter Gropius, and Le Corbusier, the high priest of the genre. By the late 1950s Cuba's modern movement had reached maturity and ushered in a mature International Style and an assimilation of a repertory of modern regionalist forms. The climax came with the 1959 revolution's political realignment, which culminated in the closing of Havana's School of Architecture in 1965.

Havana was Cuba's center of learning, culture, and architectural experimentation. By the first decades of the twentieth century the capital had three distinct districts: Old Havana, the

LEFT The cupola of the 1929 Capitolio Nacional de Cuba (National Capitol of Havana) building on a moonlit night. The Capitol was designed by Cuban architects Eugenio Raynieri, Raúl Otero, José Bens Arrate, and the Govantes y Cabarrocas architectural firm, with other architects. It was built by Purdy & Henderson. The dome was the highest point in the city until the 1950s.

RIGHT The Bank of Nova Scotia, built in 1906. In 1960 the Cuban government nationalized all eight branches of the Bank of Nova Scotia in Cuba.

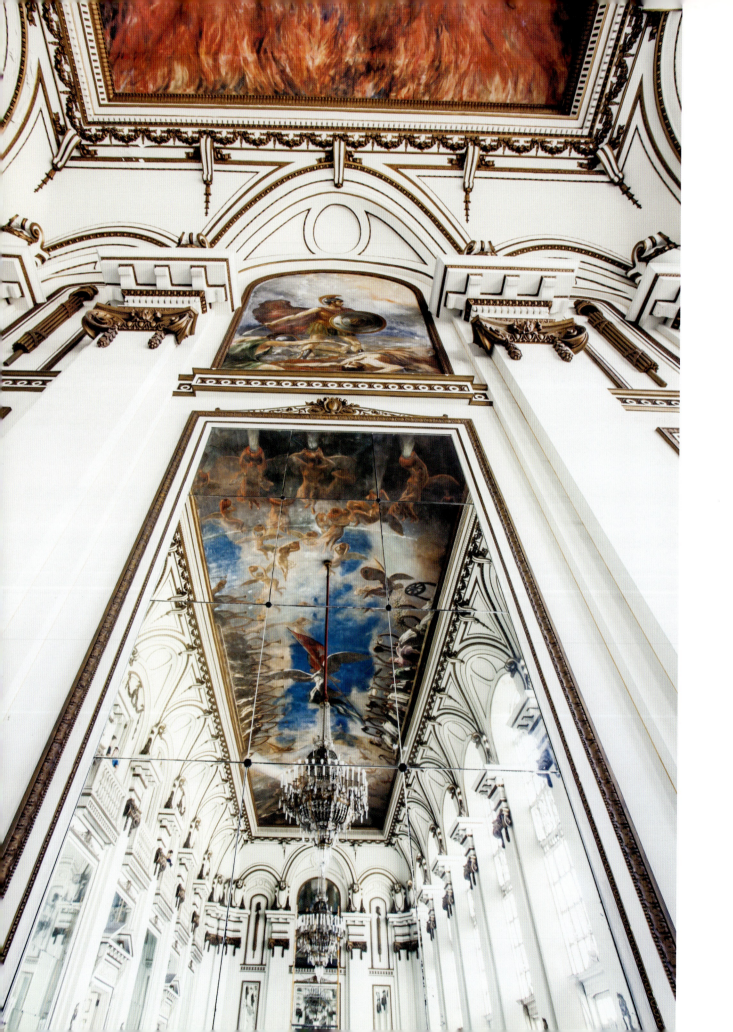

PREVIOUS Pablo González de Mendoza's house built in 1916 had Havana's first indoor swimming pool. Designed in the Pompeian style (*baño romano*), the house is currently the British ambassador's residence.

LEFT Interior of the Hall of Mirrors at the Presidential Palace, designed by Cuban architect Carlos Maruri and Belgian architect Paul Belau—who also designed the Gran Teatro de La Habana (Grand Theater of Havana)—and completed in 1920. The interior decoration was entrusted to Tiffany Studios of New York. The allegorical ceiling mural is by Cuban artist Armando García Menocal, cousin of the president of Cuba at that time, Mario García Menocal.

RIGHT Gateway to the swimming pool at the legendary Hotel Nacional, designed by the American architectural firm of McKim, Mead & White, built by the American engineering firm Purdy & Henderson, and the first building in Havana to use concrete-covered steel beams.

OVERLEAF Hotel Nacional was built because of Havana's increasing influx of bourgeois tourism and is located on the city's beautiful seaside boulevard, the Malecón. Its guest book includes celebrities such as Marlon Brando, Marlene Dietrich, Winston Churchill, Ava Gardner, Errol Flynn, Buster Keaton, Fred Astaire, Frank Sinatra and Walt Disney, among many others.

ABOVE Hotel Nacional opened on New Year's Day in 1930 and was designed by Lawrence White, Stanford White's son, in an eclectic, Spanish-Floridian resort-hotel style. Art deco architectural elements and embellishments are clearly identifiable on its towers, roof, and parapet.

four-hundred-year-old walled Spanish colonial city that today is being beautifully restored; New Havana, containing Central Havana, Vedado, and Cerro; and suburban Havana, encompassing newer developments to the south and west, due to the geographic limitations of the seacoast to the north and Havana Bay to the east.

Regardless of the proliferation of new wealth and construction, much of the earliest twentieth-century architecture was stylistically transitional and continued to pay at least partial allegiance to the historic colonial models and neoclassicism of the previous century. Reconciliation between urban architects who considered themselves early modernists and those who still thought of themselves as traditionalists resulted in a surprising outpouring of architectural styles that became known as Cuban eclecticism. The island's leading architects of the day, such as Leonardo Morales, Raúl Otero, Evelio Govantes, Félix Cabarrocas, and Eugenio Rayneri, practiced Cuban eclecticism. These men helped usher in a movement that they professed broke from the nineteenth century's colonial-style building tradition and championed a Cuban architectural Renaissance, but it was never really completely free of the pomp and empty vanity of the grand architecture of the previous century. Morales, a proponent of the new style, and who had completed his architecture studies at New York City's Columbia University in 1909, made an attempt to describe Cuban eclecticism in a 1929 *El Arquitecto* article titled "Architecture in Cuba from 1898 to 1929":

These buildings were well proportioned, but with a quasi-Greek rigidity. Later we introduced the Italian Renaissance.... After that there were some variants on Louis XVI style, and I dare say that from 1914 to 1924, our architecture was a blend of this latter style and Italian Renaissance, in a fusion that was characteristic of our country and produced many

ABOVE The mahogany and Spanish tile lobby of Hotel Nacional with all the original architectural fixtures. This hotel was immortalized in the movie *The Godfather, Part II* as the venue for the infamous 1946 gangster summit, the Havana Conference, a historic meeting of the United States Mafia and Sicilian Cosa Nostra members.

distinguished works.... The Spanish Plateresque was introduced circa 1924 and became outrageously modish for a while.... Then the Florentine came into vogue, and the California Mission, and finally at present day... Cuban colonial and new art [art deco]. The recent period has therefore spawned a plethora of styles in the absence of precise timeframes, for at the same time as one style came into fashion others that until lately had claimed the honor were still under construction.[3]

Essentially a "battle of styles," with every variation of architectural trend that was at the time considered a matter of fashion, was tried or incorporated in residential design, and because of this variety, Havana's residential architecture was said to be "splendidly encyclopedic."

An emanation of and a modernist reaction against the then fashionable art nouveau style and its gratuitous ornament was what Leonardo Morales referred to in his 1929 *El Arquitecto* article as the "new art" and has since been termed "art deco." (The name art deco is a relatively recent invention; generally describing design between the two world wars, it was effectively coined by the important exhibition *Les Années "25": Art Déco/Bauhaus/Stijl/Esprit Nouveau*, held at the Musée des Arts Décoratifs in Paris in 1966.)

The authentic *style moderne* was introduced and first made popular by the *Exposition Internationale des Arts Décoratifs et Industriels Modernes*, held in Paris in 1925. Originally, *style moderne* was used to identify decorative surface ornamentation and architectural elements, rather than a particular style of architecture. It was first thought of more as a descriptor of industrial art, based on angular, symmetrical, geometric forms, and craft decoration originating from the austere functionalism of Walter Gropius and Le Corbusier. The cleaner-lined art deco style, or *style moderne*, as it was called at the time, was associated with a wide variety of decorative arts and

PREVIOUS The richly decorated façade of the Casa de Dionisio Velasco is a confection of Beaux-Arts Spanish revival and modernist art nouveau styles and was the first grand mansion of the republican era. It was designed by Francisco Ramírez Ovando in 1912 and presently houses the Spanish Embassy.

LEFT Havana's first Manhattan-style skyscraper, the Compañía Cubana de Teléfonos (formerly the Cuban Telephone Company), was designed by Leonardo Morales and built in 1927. It was one of many buildings the Cuban architectural firm Morales & Co. built in Havana.

RIGHT The building was Havana's highest when it was built. The eclectic neo-Baroque plateresque tower is similar to that of the Telefónica building in Madrid, Spain, which was also built in the 1920s.

LEFT The Cuban Telephone Company building's Moorish (Mudéjar)-Spanish lobby ceiling is testament to Morales's reputation for reproducing traditional Cuban architectural styles and elements.

RIGHT A statue of José Martí, Cuba's national hero, in Parque Central (Central Park) and, in the distance, the historic Hotel Inglaterra (England Hotel), which was reconstructed in 1915. The Hotel Inglaterra hosted many famous people including the celebrated French actress Sarah Bernhardt.

RIGHT This Havana home's façade is an example of the flamboyant art nouveau style that Catalonian immigrants brought to Havana in the early 1900s.

luxury works produced during the interwar years. Numerous residential and public buildings in Havana adopted art deco aesthetics, ornaments, and decorations in their designs.

The art deco style was soon embellished upon, and streamline modern emerged. Streamline was popular in Havana for its blend of modernism, post-Depression pragmatism, and industrial design. Concurrent with this fashion was modern classicism, modern regionalism, and the beginnings of the International Style.

In the first half of the twentieth century the influence of modern American architecture on Havana was most prominent in the construction of the city's buildings that "scratched the sky": ten-story banks, apartment towers, hotels, warehouses, and public buildings. A few of the first examples were the more than two-hundred-foot-tall Cuban Telephone Company tower, designed by Morales y Compañiá in the eclectic taste and completed in 1927; the Hotel Sevilla, originally built in 1908 and remodeled in 1923 in a fusion of Mudejar (Moorish) tradition and twentieth-century modernism; and, most famous, the Bacardí Building, completed in 1930, with its *style moderne* decorative surface motifs strongly integrated with the edifice's interior decor.

By the mid- to late 1940s Cuba had had recurring and extended periods of economic prosperity. The island's newest architecture, now devoid of the reminders of its past colonial baroque, Mudejar, Renaissance, and Beaux-Arts traditions, began to identify itself with the International Style (a label disputed by many who believed that the modern architecture of the day transcended "style" and should be thought of more as a movement), which disseminated from Europe via the United States. Thanks to the capital investment that continued to accumulate in Cuba after World War II, Havana

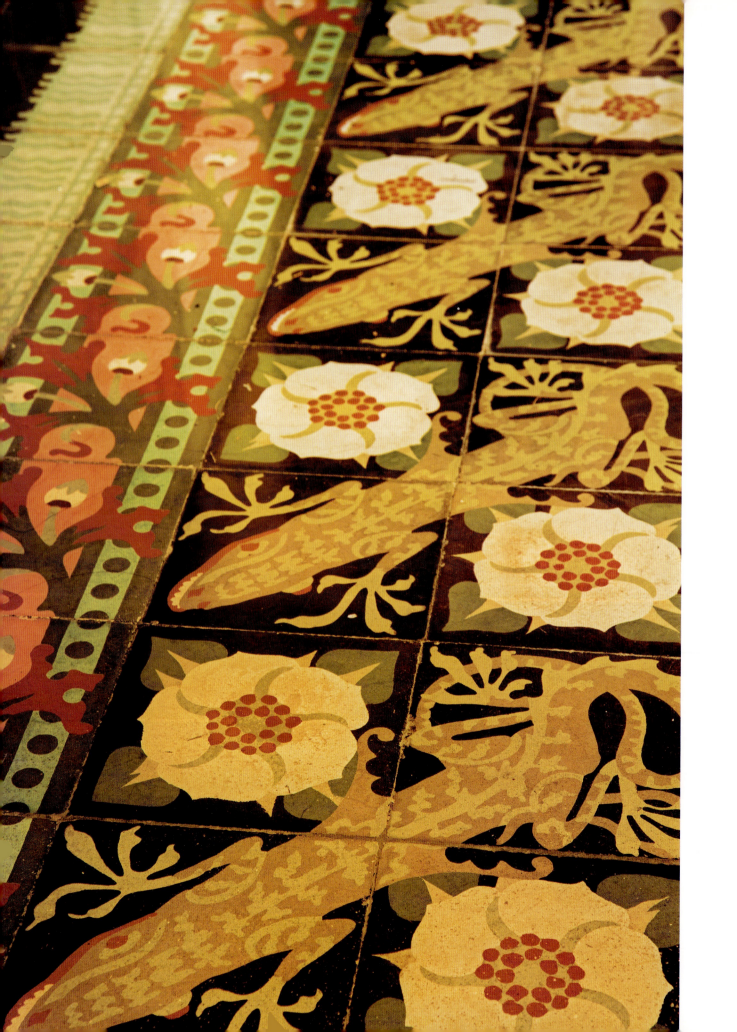

LEFT Detail of the imported art nouveau tiles in the entrance of an early twentieth-century Havana home.

ABOVE The elaborate tile "carpet" design by Luis Domenech y Montaner for the Spanish tile company Escofet y Cía gives the illusion of a hall carpet.

ABOVE/LEFT An art nouveau decorative pelican element on an Old Havana doorway.

ABOVE/RIGHT Detail of the 1910 art nouveau–style façade of Havana's El Cetro de Oro (The Golden Scepter) apartment building, named after the bakery that once occupied the ground floor and designed by Eugenio Dediot. The exquisite original wrought-iron balconies are still intact.

RIGHT This art deco alabaster sculpture is by Italian artist Dante Zoi and was commissioned during the first decade of the twentieth century. Although unauthenticated, it is said to be a depiction of the legendary femme fatale Mata Hari and is presently in one of Havana's colonial palaces: Hotel Florida.

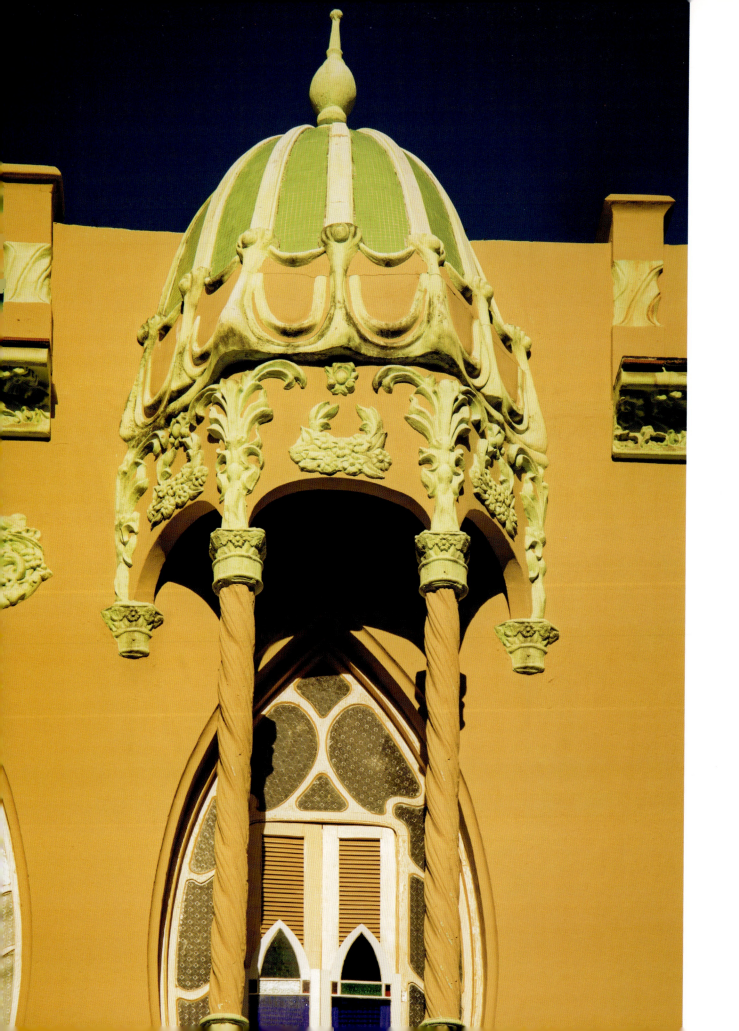

LEFT Façade detail of the Catalan modernism, or art nouveau that was popular in Havana during the first decades of the twentieth century.

RIGHT Art nouveau interior furnishings representative of the period and fashionable for Havana's emerging middle class during the early 1900s.

OVERLEAF One of the six buildings along Havana's Cárdenas Street that has similar art nouveau decorative elements and characteristics Designed in 1913 by Catalan architect Mario Rotllant, it features windows shaped like leaves, ornamented with colored glass and expressive plaster moldings with floral motifs.

ABOVE One of the many art nouveau ornamental architectural elements found throughout Havana.

RIGHT The art nouveau reception desk in Old Havana's Hotel Raquel. The hotel was designed by Venezuelan architect Naranjo Ferrer and completed in 1908.

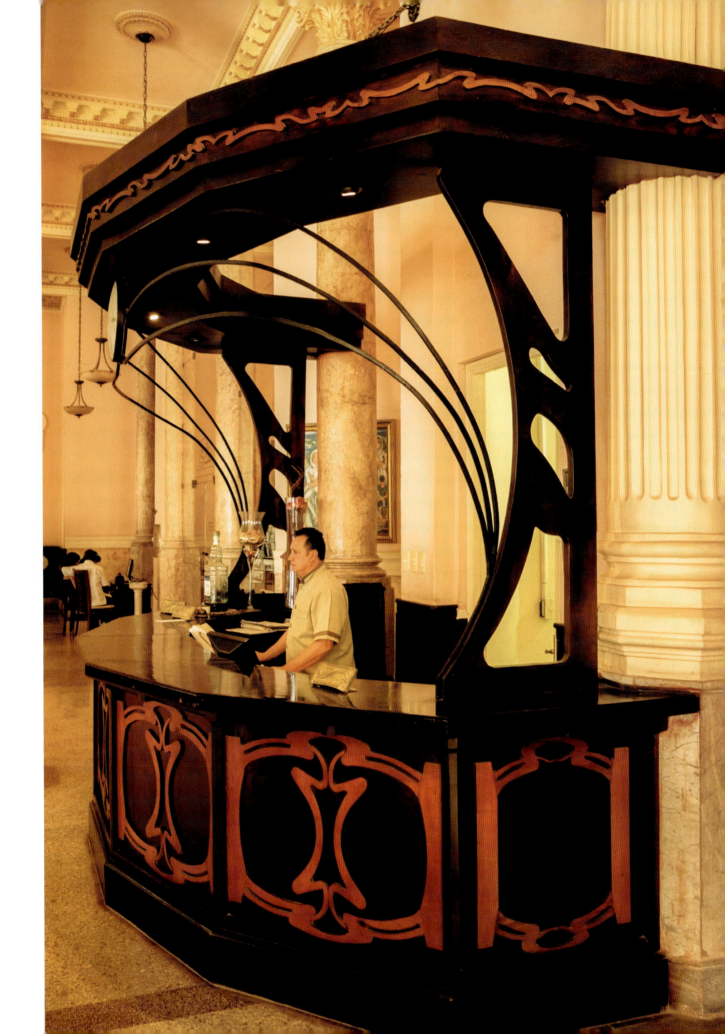

LEFT An art deco bathroom in a Vedado mansion commissioned by wealthy sugar magnate José Gómez-Mena in 1926 for his sister María Luisa, the Countess of Revilla de Camargo. Parisian firm Maison Jansen was commissioned to design the mansion's interiors.

experienced a second twentieth-century housing boom. Famous architects from around the world such as Walter Gropius, Mies van der Rohe, José Luis Sert, Franco Albini, Richard Neutra, and Philip Johnson visited Cuba, and their influence led to many International Style buildings, characterized by clean, rectilinear designs. (Both Johnson and Mies van der Rohe designed buildings for Havana that, unfortunately, were never realized.)

The International Style's geometric shapes and bare-of-ornament characteristics gave sections of Havana's modernist urban landscape the silhouette of shoe boxes on end. Fortunately, not all urban plans were carried out. One that could have been a serious detriment to the city was a project proposed by José Luis Sert, a Spanish (Catalan)-born U.S. architect and urban planner. Sert's idea was to raze major sections of Old Havana and replace antique Spanish colonial *palacios* with Le Corbusier–style skyscrapers, and to link the famous waterfront promenade, Malecón, to an artificial island with hotels, casinos, and shopping malls.

The search for new ideas in both architecture and urban planning and the technological developments of reinforced concrete, glass, and steel frames brought about a boom in the development of apartment buildings—especially for the middle classes—starting in the 1940s and continuing through the next decade. As the late Cuban historian Maria Luisa Lobo Montalvo writes, "With regard to individual housing and apartment buildings alike, two distinct architectural trends emerged: one, which we may call 'modern,' embraced new criteria of spatial distribution and functional use, but remained ultimately anodyne and expressionless. The other was more properly 'avant-garde,' and sought to generate space on

ABOVE/LEFT The bathroom features imported white, gray, and pink marble and was considered the height of luxury during the 1920s.

ABOVE/RIGHT The surrounding floor-to-ceiling mirrors and latest bathroom fixtures exhibited the extravagance that wealthy Cubans considered tasteful at the time.

RIGHT Doorway leading to the main entrance hall of Juan Pedro Baró and Catalina Lasa's 1926 Vedado residence. The open decorative iron transoms facilitate airflow through the house while also lending a touch of elegance.

LEFT The stairwell of the Baró-Lasa house with its original interior architecture and architectural fixtures has been preserved and reflects a modernist style that was avant-garde at the time.

ABOVE The early art deco style is visible in the geometric design of the colorful polished marble floors of the large entrance hall.

LEFT Glass ceiling fixture designed by René Lalique in the Palm Room, which served as a sun porch.

RIGHT Sculpture in the Baró-Lasa garden courtyard. The gardens were created by French landscape designer Jean-Claude Nicolas Forestier, the originator of Havana's Master Plan (1926–28) and designer of the Parque de la Fraternidad (Fraternity Park) surrounding the capitol.

LEFT Sand from the Nile River Basin was imported to make a special grout for the green, silver, and turquoise mosaic-tile conservatory floor and stucco walls in the Baró-Lasa house.

RIGHT This art deco house is an example of the many more modest homes that were built featuring the *style moderne* popular during this twentieth-century era.

ABOVE One of the best examples of Havana's many art deco residences is the Manuel López Chávez house designed by Esteban Rodríguez Castells and built in 1932.

ABOVE The home of Francisco Argüelles was built in 1927 in Havana's Miramar suburb and is considered the first architecturally *style moderne* house constructed in Cuba.

the basis of function. It achieved genuine heights of architectural merit by incorporating certain values of our national culture to synthesize a uniquely Cuban architecture . . ."[4]

Havana's modernity came into its glory and peaked in the 1950s, when the city's transit tunnels, large-scale hotels, airport, and modern civic center were built. Two notable works from that era are the felicitous Tribunal de Cuentas (Office of the Controller), designed and built in 1953 by Aquiles Capablanca, who employed elements derived from Le Corbusier, such as *pilotis*, or piers, which enhance the lightness of the structure, and was the stunningly original Tropicana Cabaret, a nightclub designed by Harvard University–trained Max Borges Jr. that incorporated a virtuoso spatial effect of shell vaulting set within tropical vegetation and made even more exotic by sculptures the architect created.

Thousands of homes were designed in the new modern tradition, inherited from the Cuban upper-class architecture that dictated the fashions and was destined to become the style of the petite bourgeoisie.[5] Through "cultural seepage"—that which translates the new into the popular—these homes were interpretive modernist designs built in a contemporary fashion but on a much smaller scale in the suburbs of Havana and in cities and towns throughout the island. Of course, other architectural trends surfaced in the 1950s, including modern regionalism, as seen in works by architects Ricardo Porro, Emilio del Junco, Max Borges Jr., and Mario Romañach, all of whom renewed selective colonial traditions and elements within the scope of modernism.

During the fifteen years between the end of World War II and the Cuban revolution, tourism played a major role in determining what was built and where. The relationship between tourism and Havana's mid-century architecture and urban visual culture is a different

ABOVE José Antonio Mendigutía designed the Argüelles home with both art deco exterior and interior elements. Shown here is the original front hall entrance.

and difficult study that calls for in-depth investigation beyond the scope of this book.

Although the 1959 revolution did not immediately cause a complete break with Cuba's modern architecture movement, more than two-thirds of Cuba's successful professional architects elected to leave the island. The substantive end came with the Cuban government's order in 1965 to abandon construction of the partially built National Schools of Art because of ideology. This marked a shift of focus in the direction of low-cost prefabricated housing and eventually a Soviet-style "brutalism" of rough, exposed concrete surfaces.

LEFT The recently restored art deco public school, Escuela Municipal José M. Valdés Rodríguez, in Vedado.

ABOVE/LEFT One of Havana's hundreds of modest city homes that exhibit art deco architectural detailing. This one is on San Rafael Street in Central Havana.

ABOVE/RIGHT Exterior art deco motifs on one of the building façades on Avenue Simón Bolívar in Central Havana.

LEFT The Salomon Kalmanowitz residence in the Marianao district of Havana is one of the many art deco houses in the city. It was designed by Angel López Valladares and completed in 1936.

RIGHT The Arenal Theatre's art deco design is said to make a playful reference to baroque Cuban church façades of the colonial era. The name of the cinema appears in luminous letters in the middle of the façade, reinforcing the art deco symmetry of the building.

HAVANA MODERN

While visiting Cuba in 1888, Englishman James Anthony Froude recorded an observation that typified prevalent thinking of the day: "The opinion in Cuba was, and is, that America is the residuary legatee of all the islands, Spanish and English equally, and that she will be forced to take charge of them in the end whether she likes it or not. Spain governs unjustly and corruptly. The Cubans will not rest till they are free from her, and if once independent they will throw themselves on American protection."[6]

American capital first appeared in Cuba during the third quarter of the nineteenth century as the United States began to replace Spain as Cuba's main trading partner. Spain, like most other mother countries with colonies in the Caribbean, had concentrated more on drawing revenue out of its West Indian islands than on the interests of the colonies themselves. Historically, Spanish officials had been avaricious and Spanish fiscal policy oppressive and ruinous. With the full abolition of slavery in Cuba in 1886, in addition to the great rise of sugar production and the beginnings of sugar-mill modernization, the United States deepened its economic commitment to the island. It wasn't long before the U.S. became Cuba's favorite, largest, and most important customer, especially in the sugar, tobacco, and mining sectors.

In 1898 the U.S. battleship *Maine* mysteriously exploded and sank in Havana Bay, which facilitated America's justification to intervene in the final days of Cuba's War of Independence against Spain. The U.S. went to war with Spain ostensibly to achieve Cuban freedom, but after helping win the conflict, the U.S. made sure it would dominate the island even after that. When the U.S. and Spain signed the treaty ending the war, the Cubans were not invited, and so began the first fifty-nine years of the island's twentieth-century history and a forced dependence on the U.S. In 1901 the presence of the American occupational force, with the help of the Platt Amendment, under which U.S. pressure was inserted into the new Cuban constitution in 1902, established Cuba as a virtual American protectorate. By this time, the U.S. economy had become so closely connected with Cuba that American investments totaled more than one hundred million dollars, an exorbitant sum at the time.

The U.S. intervention in Cuba's war for independence from Spain and two subsequent occupations of military rule (1898–1902 and 1906–9) paved the way for the continuing and seemingly unlimited foreign investment money, which helped fuel improvements in infrastructure and the first substantial construction boom Cuba had seen since before the wars for independence began in 1868. As Cuba expert Joseph Scarpaci points out,

> The first measures taken by the U.S. administration in Cuba between 1898 and 1902 were to establish basic infrastructure to ensure the growth of a modern city [Havana]. The United States introduced at least five major public works projects. First, it completed a network of water mains throughout the city. Second, it expanded the networks of electric streetlights, telephones, and natural gas. Third, comprehensive systems of sewage and garbage collection were established. Fourth, extended street paving ended many pitted dirt roads and would later satisfy the demands of a small number of automobile owners. Fifth, the electric streetcar replaced the horse-drawn tram running through the new neighborhood of Vedado and was gradually extended through the inner city and some suburbs.[7]

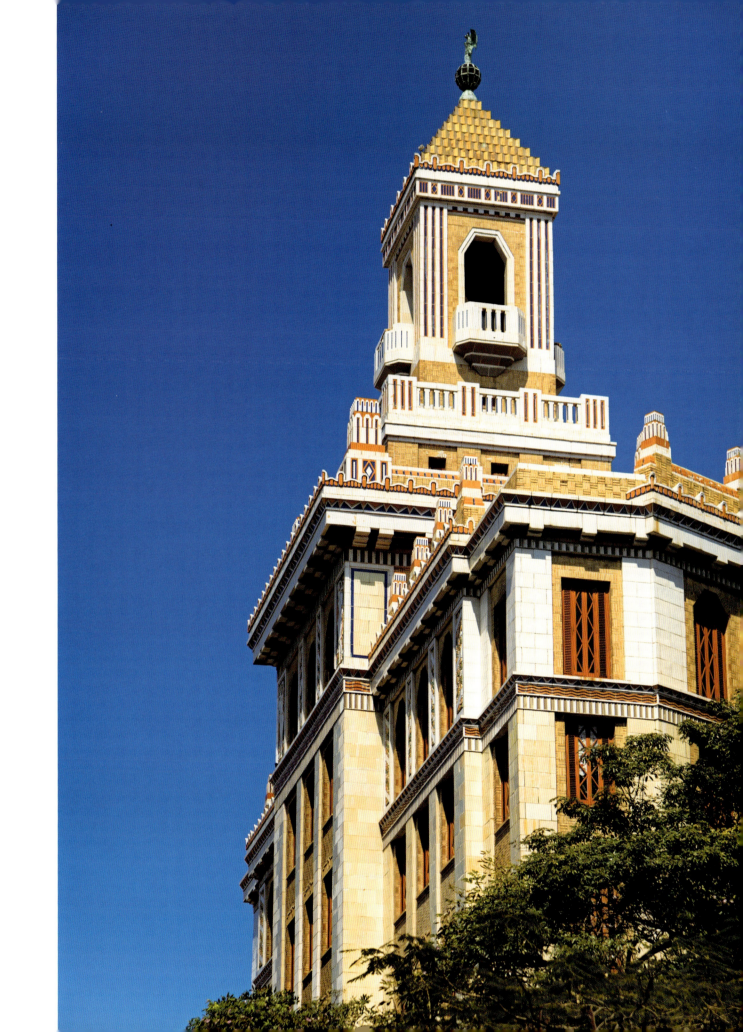

PAGE 83 The design of Havana's Bacardí building distinguishes it as one of the world's best examples of an art deco commercial building.

PREVIOUS Designed by Esteban Rodríguez Castells, Rafael Fernández Ruenes, and José Menéndez, the building was completed in 1930. Its colorful enameled terra-cotta panels of nude nymphs are by American artist Maxfield Parrish.

ABOVE The Bacardí building was the headquarters of the Bacardí rum empire. A bronze bat, a Cuban good luck emblem and the logo of the Bacardí firm, crowns the building's ziggurat-profiled top spire.

RIGHT The ground floor's exterior French-inspired art deco lines and polished Bavarian red granite serve as a perfect backdrop for the geometric brass-and-bronze lanterns.

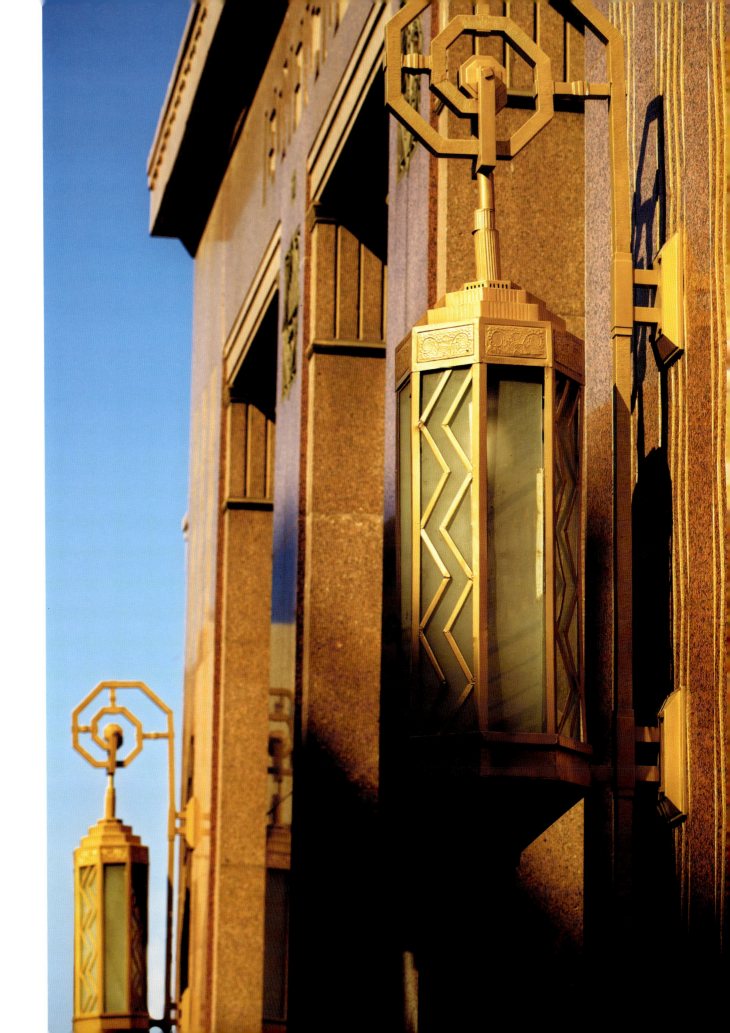

LEFT The lobby's multicolored patterned marble floors and ceiling's inverted-step design visually draw visitors into the building.

ABOVE The elevator doors have a radiant sun design, a common art deco decorative motif adapted from ancient Egypt.

OVERLEAF Rarely seen by the public, this private mezzanine bar and café was used by Bacardí executives and their friends to sample the company's rum products.

ABOVE Looking out from the mezzanine bar, the modern art deco fashion of geometrized forms and ornament is displayed.

Another positive side of the two U.S. occupations was that the hundreds of millions of dollars invested in the island revived the Cuban economy from the devastation brought about by the previous three decades of wars against Spain. Some of this money was Cuban capital that had been temporarily deposited in the U.S. during the years of conflict and returned to the island.

Along with the influx of American capital and immigration came the strong suggestive influence of North American architectural academicism. Many American architects at the time continued to follow the ideas, curriculum, and classical principles of the French-inspired Beaux-Arts style, which had become synonymous with the Gilded Age and gained more popularity with the 1893 World's Columbian Exposition, also known as the Chicago World's Fair. Outside France the Beaux-Arts style had its greatest impact in the United States, where wealthy art collectors abounded at the time in an era of eager museum building and proselytizing for the appreciation of fine and decorative arts.

Cubans continued to emulate American architectural taste, which tended to be conservative and lean toward a classical imperial style. They commissioned designs that reflected Beaux-Arts historical revivalism for their offices, hotels, railroad stations, libraries, museums, universities, and, most importantly, their homes. Other than the numerous examples of domestic architecture are Havana's early twentieth-century commercial buildings, beginning with the 1909 construction of the Lonja del Comercio (Stock Exchange), a five-story edifice (the sixth floor was added in 1939), designed by Spanish architect Tomás Mur, with a dome crowned by a bronze statue of Mercury, god of commerce. Besides the exchange itself, the building housed a bank, offices, and various stores. Across from the Lonja del Comercio on Havana Bay's waterfront is the Customs House, designed by the

ABOVE The architectural inverted-step designs and fluted pilasters with floral capitals add to the overall art deco interior.

U.S. architectural firm of Barclay Parsons & Klapp and inaugurated in 1914. Another architectural symbol of Cuba's early twentieth-century republic was Havana's monumental Central Railway Station, which was designed by another American architect, Kenneth MacKenzie Murchison, and completed in 1912. Cuba's railroad system, abandoned by the Spanish in the mid-nineteenth century, was revived, restructured, and repaired under the leadership of American William Van Horne, builder of the Canadian Pacific Railway. The project was initiated in 1900 and completed in record time in 1903; by the time Havana's railway station was built, Cuba was one of the few Latin American countries with an exceptional railway system, which reached into virtually every corner of the country until it was nationalized in 1959. Since then it has been neglected to the point of being practically nonfunctional. The design of the train station is a combination of Spanish Renaissance (the twin towers are reminiscent of La Giralda in Seville, Spain) and Beaux-Arts classicism. Other examples of the era are the residence of Dionisio Velasco, built in 1912, and the Palacio Presidencial (Presidential Palace), which was designed and built eight years later by Belgian architect Paul Belau and Cuban Carlos Maruri.

After winning its independence from Spain, Cuba was inclined to reject anything from the mother country. However, Spanish companies and associations that historically had been well established on the island didn't want to lose their foothold and influence, and so began to sponsor and support immigration and commission Spanish regional centers and social headquarters. As Cathryn Griffith writes in *Havana Revisited: An Architectural Heritage* (2010), "Subsidized mass importation of Spanish immigrants meant to 'whiten' the country deepened the control that Spanish merchants had historically exercised over urban trade."[8]

PREVIOUS Reflected in the original mirrored wall of a room adjoining the lobby are the polished bronze chandeliers and contrasting color palette that create an interplay of pure art deco architectonic aesthetics.

LEFT René Lalique designed this white marble-and-black granite art deco–style mausoleum for Juan Pedro Baró's wife Catalina Lasa in 1936. The door depicts a pair of angels with a border of the eponymous "Catalina" rose, a hybrid yellow rose that Baró had horticulturists develop especially for his bride.

ABOVE/LEFT The 1957 *La Piedad* by Rita Longa is a delicate marble bas-relief sculpture that adorns the black granite tomb of the Aguilera family in Havana's monumental Cristobal Colón Cemetery.

ABOVE/RIGHT Entrance to the Hospital de Maternidad Obrera (Workers' Maternity Hospital) built in 1940 in Havana's Marianao neighborhood by architect Emilio de Soto. The sculpture above the entrance is *Madre e Hijo* (Mother and Son) by Teodoro Ramos.

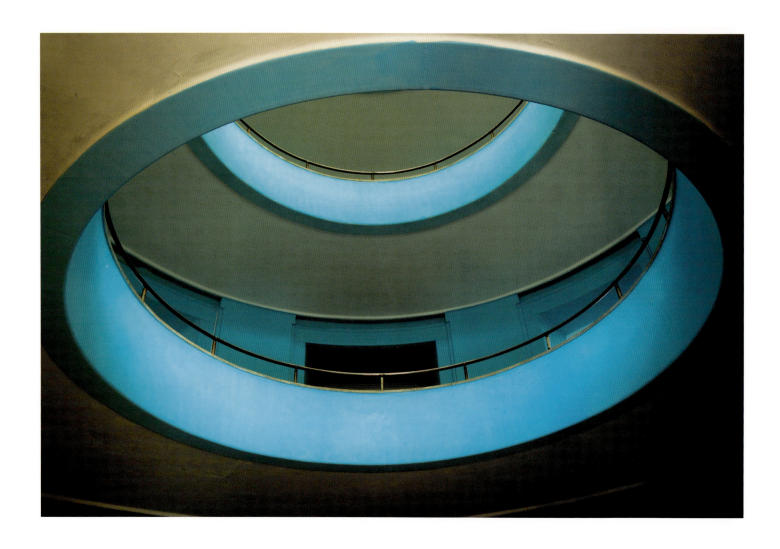

ABOVE The cathedral-like ceiling gives an exaggerated perspective to the hospital's lobby.

RIGHT The hospital's lobby mural by Enrique García Cabrera was controversial at the time it was made because it depicts a male worker of African descent among the onlookers.

OVERLEAF Interior of Iglesia de Santa Rita (Church of Saint Rita), designed by Víctor Morales and completed in 1942.

ABOVE The fourteen-story López Serrano building was designed by architects Ricardo Mira and Miguel Rosich and completed in 1932. It was Havana's first modern apartment building in the art deco style and has an exterior profile of vertical shafts and tower setbacks reminiscent of skyscrapers in Chicago and New York.

RIGHT The López Serrano building's lobby is decisively pure art deco and is considered to be a paradigm of artistic and technological modernity in Cuban architecture.

Traditionally, Castilians and Andalusians were the Spanish regional groups that predominated in the colonial founding and settlement of Cuba, but by the nineteenth century Galicians, Asturians, and Basques outnumbered them and prevailed. Examples of the new structures meant to serve these groups were the Palacio de la Asociación de Dependientes del Comercio (Palace of the Association of Store Clerks), built in 1907 and used as a central headquarters for Spanish regional societies; the Casino Español, an association formed by Spanish immigrants, which was completed in 1914; and the Centro Gallego, which housed Havana's Galician community and was inaugurated in 1915. The Asturian Society's enormous four-story Centro Asturiano opened its doors in 1927 and incorporated one of Cuba's most elaborate stained-glass ceilings above its grand staircase.

MODERNISMO

With the influx of Spanish immigrants came the introduction of *modernismo*, or art nouveau style. (A distinction can be made between *modernismo* and *modernisme* the Spanish and Catalan versions of art nouveau.) This decorative style originated in the late nineteenth century in Europe and flourished for a short while in America in the early twentieth century. Whether it was called *art belle epoque* or *art fin de siècle* in France; *modernismo* in Spain; *modernista* in Catalonia (a distinction can be made between *modernismo* and *modernista*); *Sezessionstil* in Austria and Hungary; *stile Liberty*, *stile floreale*, or *arte nuova* in Italy; *Jugendstil* in Germany; or art nouveau in England and America, the movement offered no new construction techniques and did not have a long life, ending with World War I.

LEFT The lobby's red Moroccan marble walls, geometric patterns, and radial design of the crushed-stone floor tiles emphasize directional movement toward the elevator and stairs.

RIGHT Detail of the ornamental enamel and polished nickel-silver sheeting relief panel *El Tiempo* (The Time) by Enrique García Cabrera. The panel depicts a clock, three airplanes, and a running figure, together symbolizing the obsession with time and the speed of the world's mechanization during this twentieth-century period.

LEFT Enrique García Cabrera's Vedado house was designed by Harvard-educated Max Borges Jr. García Cabrera, who studied art in Paris and Rome, designed the relief sculpture on the façade's second floor. He was a graphic artist, painter, professor, and former director of the National School of Fine Arts San Alejandro.

RIGHT The kitchen's simplicity remains unchanged since the house was built.

OVERLEAF García Cabrera's studio. Cabrera was one of Cuba's most famous graphic artists and designed many art deco covers for the Cuban style magazines *Carteles* and *Bohemia*. The tile floor has a dashed (*jaspeado*) surface application where the tiles were painted to give a marbled surface effect.

LEFT An art deco staircase leading to the second-floor bedrooms.

RIGHT The living room with its hinged mahogany cupboard, which swings out to reveal a small lavatory and powder room.

ABOVE The Rodríquez Vázquez apartment tower, better known as the Teatro América (American Theatre) building. It was designed by architects Fernando Martínez Campos and Pascual de Rojas with contrasting green-and-white vertical setbacks and recessed windows, which epitomize the streamline *style moderne*, a late phase of art deco.

Although it never became widespread in Cuba, it was the beginning of an aesthetic that consciously set out to revolutionize design in interiors and architecture. The few examples of art nouveau's legacy in Havana are found not only in architecture but also in carpentry, ceramic floor tiles, stained glass, furniture, and book and magazine illustration. The sensuous curvilinear, flowerlike designs, such as those of the ironwork over the entrances to the Paris Métro, influenced and were responsible for initiating a general rejection of late-nineteenth-century architectural historicism while coinciding with the Beaux-Arts Cuban eclecticism that continued to be popular. In America, Louis Comfort Tiffany was the leading proponent of the style and was commissioned to create stained-glass windows for commercial shops in Havana and elaborate lamps and colorful stained-glass window designs for the residences of wealthy patrons throughout the city. Many exponents of art nouveau architecture can be found today on Cárdenas and Manrique Streets in Havana. Another prime example of Cuban art nouveau can be seen in the various decorative façade treatments of the Palacio Cueto, completed in 1908 and currently undergoing renovation and restoration. Art nouveau architecture often degenerated into simply exterior and/or interior decoration, as in Havana's El Cetro de Oro (The Golden Scepter) apartment building, constructed in 1910, with its elegantly decorative façade, sixteen-foot ceilings, and imported marble floors. It was free from the late-nineteenth-century historical models and was a transitory step toward emancipation from École des Beaux-Arts architectural designs and methods. By the end of World War I, the influences of the art nouveau movement had ended in Cuba but had led to a more symmetrical, geometric style that came to be known as art deco. Art deco developed as a reaction against the elaborate, sinuous fluidity of art nouveau and

ABOVE The building's ground floor. Teatro América is the Caribbean's best-preserved art deco movie theatre. Above the theatre were offices, shops, private apartments and a restaurant.

moved toward architectural elements with flat, bare surfaces and the sterner lines of machinery. Art deco's central characteristics are sharp edges, clean lines, and stylish symmetry.

⚜ ⚜ ⚜

In the mid-1920s, after two decades of independence from Spain, Cuba continued to enjoy American investment, and sugar prices soared. Havana shops "bulged with North American manufactured goods—radios, refrigerators, and sewing machines, all the appurtenances of the modern age."[9] Havana had a higher standard of living than any other Caribbean city and was better off than most in Latin America. The period eventually became popularly known as the *danza de los millones* (dance of the millions), and an even more aggressive building momentum was initiated throughout the island, this time with a stronger overture toward modernization and the development of a more modern architecture. The architectural content in Havana and other Cuban cities became more diversified across the spectrum of public and private offices and institutions, government buildings, bars and restaurants, hotels, hospitals, social clubs, and commercial complexes.

During Cuba's prosperous "fat-cow" (*vaca gorda*) period, from 1914 to the early 1920s, when sugar prices were high, the new elite spent a great deal of money on the construction of domestic architecture.[10] Because the old and central parts of Havana had become increasingly crowded and lacked some of the more modern domestic conveniences, the aspirational nouveaux riches sought to imitate the island's wealthiest families by building their seafront or palatial homes in El Vedado and Miramar, areas farther to the west of the city, especially after World War I. They commissioned what they believed to be the latest in fashion and in the "best of taste."

PREVIOUS The theatre's original moderne interior fixtures and furniture have been preserved, as shown here in the second floor ladies' cloakroom.

LEFT Hallway seating and the double-curved staircase leading to second-floor balcony seats.

ABOVE/LEFT Colorful, original etched-glass panels are featured throughout the theatre.

ABOVE/RIGHT The theatre's interior features cantilevered box seating that offers an unobstructed view of the stage and movie screen.

OVERLEAF The theatre's stage is designed in the form of a seashell and the auditorium seats more than a thousand.

ABOVE The lobby's multicolored terrazzo floor features zodiac motifs that encircle a map of the Americas.

RIGHT Detail of the lobby floor, Sagittarius's zodiac sign.

Others invested their profits in handsome mansions in Havana, dispatching their large families to Rome, Paris and London and themselves purchasing lavish cars. They and their families returned to attempt to re-create in the Vedado the architecture of the Italian Renaissance, laced by the style of Louis XVI, or even Florentine Gothic; towers, miradors, minarets, replaced flat roofs—the Villa Medici everywhere, bankers of the new world pursuing the idiosyncrasies of their predecessors. The Vedado became a very metropolis of marble palaces, while a sumptuous new suburb, Miramar, with houses with large gardens, sprang up across the Almendares River, facing the ocean.[11]

In Vedado, Cuban architect Leonardo Morales designed and built a large home in 1916 for banker and landowner Pablo González de Mendoza. The monumental house was surrounded by large gardens that ensured privacy and contained romantic marble sculptures and fountains throughout. The most famous feature of this neoclassical house is the Roman-style pool, which is reminiscent of a Pompeian impluvium. Equipped with a wooden Mudejar ceiling, often found in Cuban colonial architecture, it was the first indoor swimming pool built in Havana. In terms of domestic architecture, the eclectic "Vedado Villa" styles dominated in the neighborhood and rivaled any suburban area in the world's great cities for the display of luxury dwellings.

It should be remembered that by the mid-1920s the island had once again managed to become one of the world's wealthiest tropical nations; Havana joined the ranks of the great world capitals and became known as the "jewel in the Caribbean crown." Although there was no one, discernible trend in domestic architecture, Havana distinguished itself as being enviably stylish. As Cuban writer Alejo Carpentier put it,

LEFT A Vedado apartment building's staircase with the sensual curvilinear lines popular in the period.

ABOVE A view of the Vedado apartment building's lobby's circular stairwell that displays an exaggerated perspective.

ABOVE The Cine-Teatro Sierra Maestra (formally the Teatro Lutgardita) was designed by the firm of Govantes and Cabarrocas and opened in 1932. The theatre interiors exemplify an attempt to fuse art deco with regional identity styles, in this case exotic Mayan-temple themes.

RIGHT A general view of the theatre interior with a pair of pre-Columbian fantasy temples on either side of the stage.

OVERLEAF A view from the balcony showing the stage, orchestra section, and audience seating. The sidewall mural painted by Fernando Tarazona represents a Central American landscape.

RIGHT Rafael de Cárdenas designed this sculptural streamline moderne white-and-black chevron-patterned staircase for pharmaceutical heiress Hilda Sarra's house in 1941.

The superpositioning of styles, the innovation of styles, good and bad, more often bad than good, went into creating this *style without style* in Havana, which, in the long run, through symbiosis, through amalgamation, has imposed a strange baroquism that replaces any style, filling a new page in the history of urban behavior. Because, little by little, from these ill-assorted combinations, from the mélanges, from the flinging together of different realities, sprout the lasting features of the overall idiosyncrasy that distinguishes Havana from other cities in the continent.[12]

Unfortunately, Cuba's early twentieth-century prosperity mostly benefited the already wealthy sugar barons, banks, and industrial monopolies on the island and was characterized by political and administrative corruption and the waste or theft of public funds. Vast swaths of land, predominantly sugarcane fields, gradually reverted to large United States corporations. The United Fruit Company was one of many American firms that purchased Cuban land for a pittance. Although the hundreds of millions of dollars that American companies invested in mining, railroad, tobacco, coffee, Cuban industries, and most of all sugar paid for massive civic constructions and improved public utilities, the projects proved to be popular predominantly with the small percentage of Havana's fashionable society and American tourists. As the historian Richard Gott explains, "Cuba had become a significant producer of immense wealth, in whose activities American companies and individuals were deeply involved. Bankers and traders, mill and plantation owners, railroad operators and simple investors, all looked to the United States to protect their interests. Cuba had become a colony in all but name."[13]

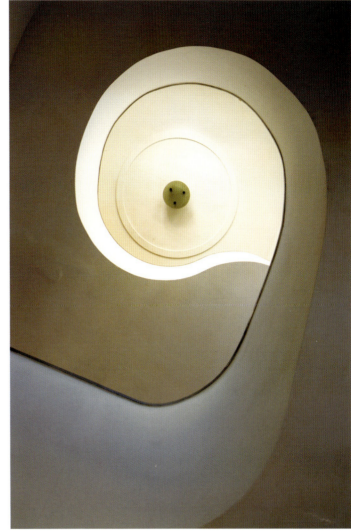

LEFT The Hilda Sarra residence is a combination of streamline moderne and Le Corbusier's rationalist design that results in a unique Cuban modernist form, partially because it was built in 1934 and added to in 1941.

ABOVE/LEFT A view of the stairwell windows of the winding art deco staircase.

ABOVE/RIGHT The serpentine staircase becomes an abstract form when viewed from the ground up.

ABOVE Situated on the Malecón, the art deco–inspired Casa de las Américas building was constructed in 1959, months after the triumph of the Cuban revolution.

RIGHT The Casa de las Américas employs geometric vertical lines and setbacks that are characteristic of the streamline art deco architecture so popular in Havana two decades earlier.

LEFT The Fausto Theatre, designed by Saturnino Parajón, faces the Paseo del Prado, the most picturesque treelined boulevard in Havana. The theatre was built over the foundations of an old theatre of the same name and completed in 1938. Parajón was awarded the Architectural Association's Gold Medal Prize for his design in 1941.

ABOVE Detail of the clean, art deco molded-cement lines of the Fausto Theatre, where theatre, dance, and musical performances are scheduled throughout the week.

ABOVE The Netherlands Embassy in Havana's Miramar neighborhood. A mid-twentieth-century home that was restored and renovated by Cuban architect Jose Antonio Choy in 2013.

RIGHT Interior of the Netherlands Embassy.

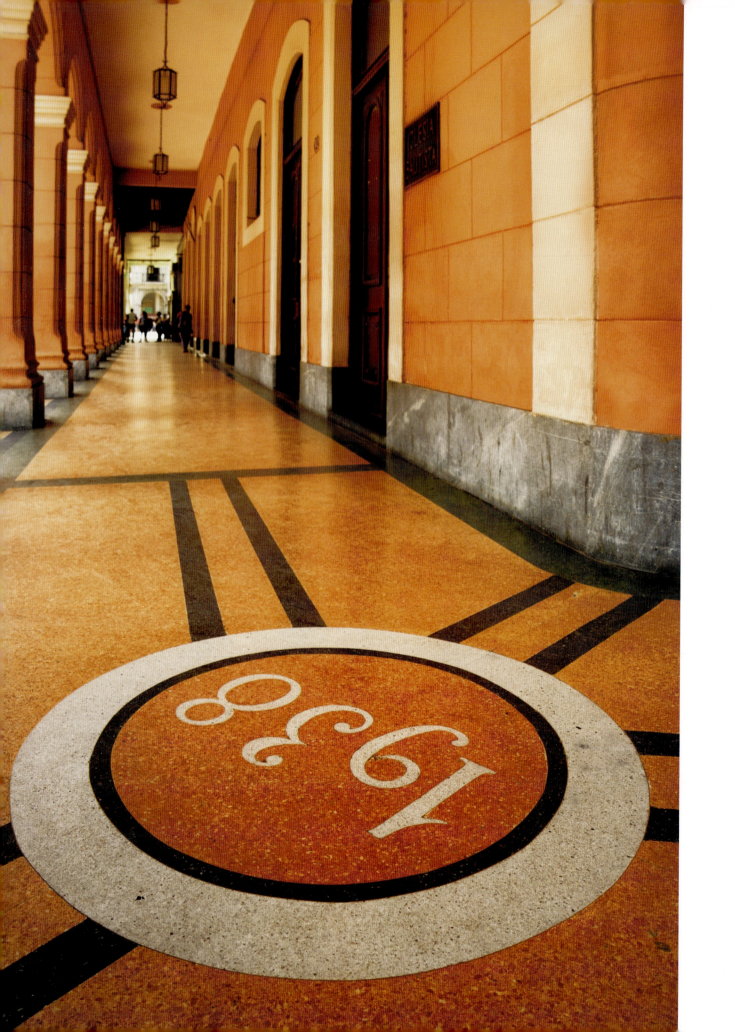

LEFT This mid-twentieth-century arcade exemplifies the architectural tradition of colonnade and portico construction popular throughout 450 years of Cuban architectural history.

ABOVE La Moderna Poesía bookstore was originally a Cuban publishing house owned by José López Serrano and built in 1935.

ABOVE Interior aluminum railing balcony of Havana's Colegio de Arquitectos (College of Architects) designed by Fernando de Sárraga and Mario Esquiroz and built in 1947.

RIGHT The College's lobby, or great hall, has a large vertical three-story floor window for natural light as well as a continuously curving staircase, both of which add to the geometric elegance of the interior design.

Because centuries of colonial Spanish corruption of favor trading and backroom dealing had been firmly embedded in the bureaucratic habits and "way of doing business," the new independent republic that Cubans had fought for failed to create a credible political system. By the mid-1920s U.S. officials mostly served as shadow advisors to a series of corrupt Cuban presidents brought to power through fraudulent elections. Ironically, the omnipresent influence of American economics helped to prompt the growing contingency of wealthy Cubans, and social conventions were in flux, symbolizing evolving social and cultural attitudes. The nouveau-riche self-appointed oligarchy was unlike the landowning nobles of the Spanish colonial era. They considered their common background of new money, pseudo-culture, manners, and ostentatious taste the equivalent of a class of suburban aristocracy. Their exploitations of Cuba of this era were very similar to what others had done elsewhere in Latin America, for example, the Minor Keith family, who built railroads in Costa Rica and a banana empire to support it; the oil speculators and drillers of Venezuela; or the Guggenheims, who developed silver and copper mines in Mexico and South America. In fact, American interests owned between one-quarter and one-third of Cuba's best land by this time. "During the 1915–1925 boom of the sugar industry, U.S. capital took control of several strategic sectors of the Cuban economy: besides sugar, it took control of mining, public services, banking, foreign debt and land. They almost entirely owned the electricity and telephone companies, numerous energy industries (charcoal, oil, alcohol); as well as most of the railroad; cement, tobacco and canned food factories."[14]

⚜ ⚜ ⚜

PREVIOUS The 1944 reinforced-concrete Solimar (Sun and Sea) apartment building in Central Havana, designed by Manuel Copado, is an example of expressionist modern architecture. The wide circular balconies represent ocean waves, and in turn celebrate the Caribbean Sea.

ABOVE Cine Astral in Centro Habana was built in a late-streamline art deco style and opened in 1950 with a seating capacity of 2,400.

RIGHT This streamline moderne apartment building was designed by Críspulo Goizueta and built in 1941. It is transitional in style as the bulbous art deco balconies are coupled with the rationalist design practice of no extraneous decorative elements.

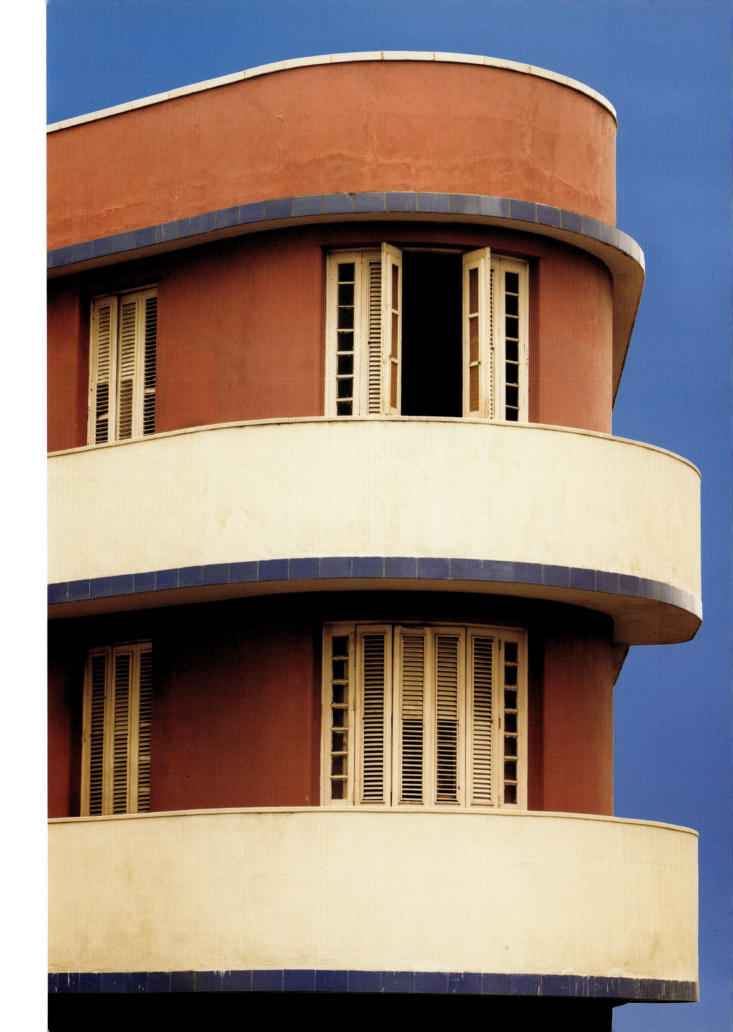

LEFT There was a strong Jewish community in Havana, numbering more than 15,000, until the 1959 revolution when 90 percent of Cuban Jewry fled the island overnight. Today there are fewer than a thousand Jews in Havana but the Hebrew Community Building in Vedado, which was designed by Aquiles Capablanca and built in 1953, continues to operate. The majority of the interiors are original, as seen in this ground-floor hallway.

RIGHT Capablanca is most famous for designing the huge Ministry of the Interior building on Plaza de la Revolución, also in 1953. His Hebrew Community Building incorporates a synagogue, administrative offices, a library, and an auditorium. This entrance to the auditorium displays the geometric patterns that demonstrate modernity.

ABOVE Renovations with extensive repairs were carried out and so today the building looks much the same as it did in 1953 when it opened.

RIGHT Visually, Capablanca's spiral staircase design has an abstract Escher-like modernist aesthetic.

LEFT Emilio Fernández pursued a structuralist approach when he designed the Anti-Blindness League building in 1959. The decorative brick-textured surfaces illustrate an architectural imagination unusual for the late 1950s.

Between the end of World War I and the onset of the Great Depression there were worldwide revolutions in art, fashion, literature, musical taste, and social mores. The Havana editors of the bilingual glossy monthly magazine *Social*, founded in 1916, which catered to and chronicled the lifestyles of a specific audience of erudite, cosmopolitan elite, explained their objective as one that was "dedicated to describing our great social events, art exhibits, and fashion shows by means of the pencil or the camera lens."[15] The content of the publication, nevertheless, was of a much broader scope. It included sections on Cuban architecture, interior decoration, high fashion, and design, as well as reviews of social events. *Social* was published until 1933, with two short revival periods, the last of which was in 1938. During its life the magazine was the epitome of the avant-garde and the voice of modernity, covering art nouveau, art deco, cubism, and futurism; it was considered the arbiter of taste and culture and the most prominent forecaster of fashion on the island. Every month during the first period of the magazine, *Social* published an architectural art page titled "Arte Arquitectonico" that pictured one of Havana's mansions, featuring exterior and interior photography and the architect or architectural firm responsible for the design. In a 1917 issue an advertisement, playing to *Social*'s image-conscience consumers, boasted that in proportion Havana had more automobiles than any other city in the world. "At the end of the 1920s the art deco design invaded the magazine with large straight planes that cut and superimposed upon themselves, forming sharp edges."[16]

Havana's new caste of bankers, "sugarcrats," and rich industrialists had replaced the Spanish and Creole aristocracy, many of

ABOVE All four sides of the rectangular League building have unexpected façade designs or decorative treatments.

RIGHT Detail of the unique brick-textured surface design at one end of the building.

LEFT The 1957 house of Eugenio Leal was designed by Eduardo Canas Abril and Nujim Nepomechie who, influenced by the architecture of Oscar Niemeyer (who visited Cuba), combined the main rectangular block with a curvilinear vault.

RIGHT One of Havana's most celebrated architects, Mario Romañach designed this house for Guillermina de Soto Bonavia in 1957. The use of bare bricks and wood screens projecting from the brick façade are characteristic of Romañach's buildings.

OVERLEAF The huge, curved theatre marquee was formerly part of the Radiocentro Building, where the Cuban headquarters of Warner Brothers opened in 1947. Renamed Yara Cinematography Cultural Center and headquarters of the Cuban Radio and Television Institute, it is today home to film festivals and other cultural events.

ABOVE The 1953 Odontological Building's architect, Antonio Quintana, was awarded the College of Architects' Gold Medal for his design. The façade's patterned sunshade (*brise-soleil*) structure was first popularized in modern architecture by Le Corbusier.

whose members had succumbed to indebtedness or insolvency. The new haute bourgeoisie had little training in how to be patrons of the arts or culture; the best these citizens could manage was to imitate the old guard in displays of their own interpretations of grandeur. *Social* magazine proved to be a relevant and important part of Havana's sociocultural fabric, serving as a guide for the nouveaux riches and a gauge for taste that helped to curb and/or refine the ostentatious spending of newly found wealth.

It was said that no other city in the world had proportionately as large a wealthy population as Havana and for those who visited Cuba few could contain their astonishment at the spectacle of opulence. "Cubans spend money with both hands," commented a visitor, "and they could teach us Americans about the art of extravagance in the construction of beautiful houses and the purchase of jewelry, clothing from Paris, and large automobiles." U.S. consul Carlton Hurst recalled: "Everybody in Cuba had money. . . . People started to erect sumptuous villas in Country Club Park, Almendares and elsewhere; magnificent automobiles were imported from the north."[17]

⚜ ⚜ ⚜

No longer was Cuba's architecture equated with baroque or neoclassical styles. Cuban architects began to look to the "new art," *style moderne*, and beyond, which was emblematic of the rising new era and reflected the progress generated by a finely tuned industrial revolution and the evolution of society. This new class of Cuban entrepreneurs belonged to exclusive tennis, sailing, and beach clubs, such as the Havana Yacht Club, and commissioned architects and interior decorators to design homes that broke from the neoclassical

ABOVE The Odontological lobby's fresco mural, *El Dolor Humano* (The Human Pain), was painted by Mariano Rodríguez, whose work focused on the essence of being Cuban.

eclecticism of the century's first thirty years. Status-symbol spending by wealthy Cubans began to favor modernist fashion.

The modern movement started to make its mark in Cuba during the mid- to late 1920s, through the influence of *style moderne* or art deco. It is important here to point out that art deco was not *the* style during these interwar years; it was only *a* style, and modernism (particularly in Europe and the U.S.) was equally strong, and in the end lasted much longer. To understand fully the distinction between art deco and modernism, it is necessary to examine their beginnings and trace their development. Like all styles and periods in art history, a style is either an embellishment upon a preceding style or a reaction against it. As discussed earlier, art deco grew out of a reaction against the eccentricities of art nouveau and evolved from traditional ideas of design and ornament. Modernism's birth was different. It was less a style than a movement and was not so much evolutionary as revolutionary. It actually began in the nineteenth century during the Industrial Revolution with such architectural technological advances and experiments as Gustave Eiffel's iron bridges and 1889 skeletal tower and Joseph Paxton's 1851 prefabricated iron-and-glass Crystal Palace. Architects and designers who adopted the art deco style copied and adapted the geometric shapes, planes, and lines of cubism and applied them to architectural elements and ornament. Modernist architects theorized about and pursued the dissection and analysis of form and applied these things three-dimensionally, just as the cubists did on canvas. Art deco was essentially a French style, whereas modernism was international. As early as the late 1920s the latter was called by some the "International Style" and by others "functionalism."

While Havana continued to extricate itself from the Beaux-Arts American mansion style, a more modern vocabulary appeared

LEFT The FOCSA building (Fomento de Obras y Construcciones, S.A.) contains 400 individual family apartments and is loosely based on a Le Corbusian model. It was completed in 1956, and at the time was considered one of the largest reinforced-concrete structures in the world.

ABOVE One of the best examples of progressive Cuban modernist architecture is the house that Max Borges Jr. designed and built for himself in 1950. This sophisticated rectangular box perched on *piloti* is considered one of Havana's quintessential modernist houses and a salute to Le Corbusier's International Style.

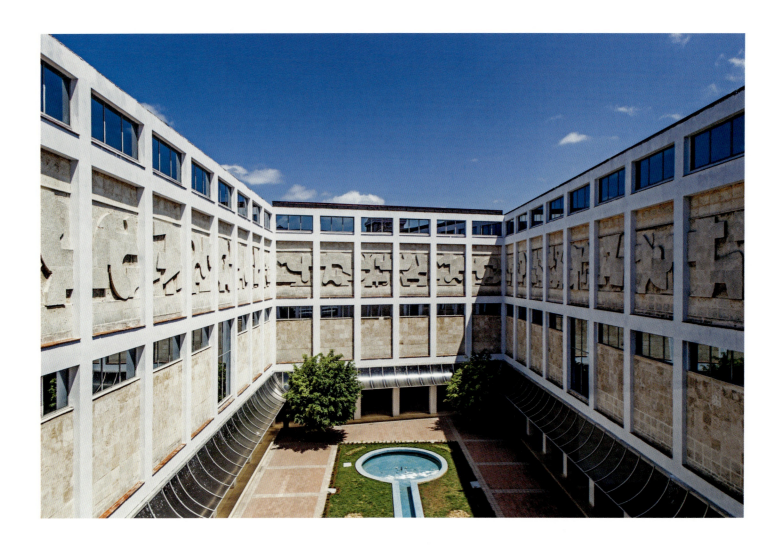

ABOVE Interior courtyard of the National Cuban Fine Arts Museum, designed by Alfonso Rodríguez Pichardo and opened in 1954.

RIGHT Sculpture completed in 1953 by Ernesto González-Jerez on the sidewall of the museum.

OVERLEAF Formerly the Teatro Blanquita and originally owned by politician Alfredo Hornedo, who named it after his first wife, Blanca Maruri, it opened on December 30, 1949, with the production of Lou Walters's *From Paris to New York*. The seating capacity of 6,730 made it the largest cinema in the world and host to many famous entertainers. It was renamed Karl Marx Theatre after the 1959 revolution and continues as a cinema, live theatre, and concert venue today.

ABOVE Max Borges Jr. designed the Paula Maza house, which is one of the hundreds of more modest modernist residences in Havana.

and progressed at a steady pace. Art deco's sleek, geometric lines conveyed elegance and sophistication and seemed to celebrate a technological machine age, gathering momentum as it developed. The term "art deco," however, is not used to describe a specific style of architecture, but rather applies to interior design, the decorative arts, and specific architectural ornamentations

The first Havana home incorporating art deco decorative motifs was Juan Pedro Baró's. Although Cuban architects Evelio Govantes and Félix Cabarrocas designed the 1926 house in a Beaux-Arts Italian Renaissance style, the dwelling was unique among Vedado mansions in adopting moderne aesthetics in its interior embellishments, boasting decorations by French designer René Lalique. Another example of an early art deco interior is that of the Palacio de la Condesa de Revilla de Camargo, a two-story French classical revival mansion completed in 1927 and built of Capellanía stone. The countess, a great benefactress of the arts in Cuba, commissioned Maison Jansen of Paris to design the interior of her home, which included a pink, white, and black marble master bathroom, a tour de force of moderne execution. In 1927 the home of Francisco Argüelles was built in Havana's Miramar suburb and it is considered the first architecturally modern-style house constructed in Cuba. Other noteworthy examples of art deco influences are scattered throughout Havana in both residential and commercial buildings, the most famous of which is the French-influenced Bacardí Building, completed in 1930, with its colorful Maxfield Parrish terra-cotta panels.

Beginning in the second half of the 1920s the French landscape architect, urban planner, and *conservateur des promenades de Paris* Jean-Claude Nicolas Forestier was invited to Havana to work with a team of Cuban engineers and architects to transform Havana's Spanish colonial image into a metropolitan vision of the new republic.

ABOVE The 1959 interior of the Enrique Borges house showing the indoor-outdoor living concept made popular during the 1950s. Enrique was an architect and Max Borges Jr.'s brother, with whom he collaborated on many design projects.

The objective was to draw up an overall plan to link metropolitan Havana's dispersed locations into harmonious park systems and land use, based on the type Baron Georges-Eugène Haussman enacted in Paris in the nineteenth century. One of the project's Cuban engineers described the proposed plan thus, which was ideally to include

> ... a series of boulevards, avenues, streets, and walkways that interconnecting with existing ones would facilitate interurban movement as well as expand the increase of the city's activity and beauty, giving it squares, plazas, open areas, and parks for the people to enjoy. This would also improve on the decongestion of commercial districts, creating connections with the existing streets and roads that link the city centers of agricultural and industrial population.[18]

The Depression's economic crisis, Forestier's death in 1930, and the fall from office of Cuba's president at the time, Gerardo Machado (1925–33), meant that Forestier's master plan would never be fully realized. Still, numerous improvements were accomplished during the five years of its implementation. These included enlarging the Paseo del Prado and extending the grounds and parks surrounding the Capitolio Nacional (National Capitol Building) with the adjoining Parque de la Fraternidad. Forestier also landscaped the Avenida de los Presidentes with its statue of Cuba's first president, Tomás Estrada Palma. Thought by many to be Forestier's greatest achievement was his design for Havana's waterfront promenade, the Malecón, as it is in its present form, which he modeled after the Costanera Sur in Buenos Aires, another of his projects. Forestier's plan was a major contribution that helped define Havana as the beautiful, uniquely classic, and somewhat modern city it is today.

By the late 1930s the art deco movement had drawn to a close and other variants, such as the American streamline style and modern regionalism, appeared, causing disagreement among many of

LEFT The twenty-one story Hotel Riviera was designed in 1957 by Miami architect Igor Polevitzky for mobster Meyer Lansky, and it was Havana's first hotel with central air conditioning. The project was originally given to architect Philip Johnson and named the Hotel Mónaco. The sculpture of a sea horse and mermaid is by Rolando López Dirubes and is original to the hotel's *porte cochere*.

ABOVE Hotel Riviera's reception desk, where celebrities of the day, including Ginger Rogers, Ava Gardner, Nat King Cole, Frank Sinatra, William Holden, and many others, checked in.

ABOVE The Riviera's L'Aiglon fine dining restaurant with the original festive mural by Hipólito Hidalgo de Caviedes showing Cubans in costumes during carnival.

RIGHT A detail of Hidalgo de Caviedes's mural and one of the original 1957 restaurant chandeliers.

LEFT The Riviera's saltwater pool, where Esther Williams performed, was the largest in Havana and was surrounded by seventy-five changing cabañas, each one with two dressing rooms and a private telephone.

ABOVE Swinging front doors of the Hotel Riviera, which had been open less than two years when Fidel Castro held a press conference there in 1959. A year later he nationalized all Cuba's hotel-casinos.

ABOVE The abstract bas-relief sculpture was designed by Rolando López Dirube and covers the wall that led to the casino. Originally Philip Johnson appointed Wilfredo Lam to be the mural artist. During Johnson and Lam's initial meeting with Meyer Lansky (Johnson's only visit to Havana), Lansky instructed Lam to include a pair of large dice in the mural, whereupon Philip Johnson said to Lansky, "Don't be so crude." Both Johnson and Lam were fired on the spot.

RIGHT Much of the original furniture and sculpture is still found throughout the hotel. Los Angeles decorator Albert Parvin designed the interiors with custom-made furniture and commissioned sculptures by Cuban artists.

OVERLEAF *Ritmo Cubano* (Cuban Rhythm) by Florencio Gelabert is a large bronze sculpture that commands the hotel lobby and depicts a couple dancing. Hotel Riviera is one of Havana's last architectural landmarks to be built before the 1959 revolution.

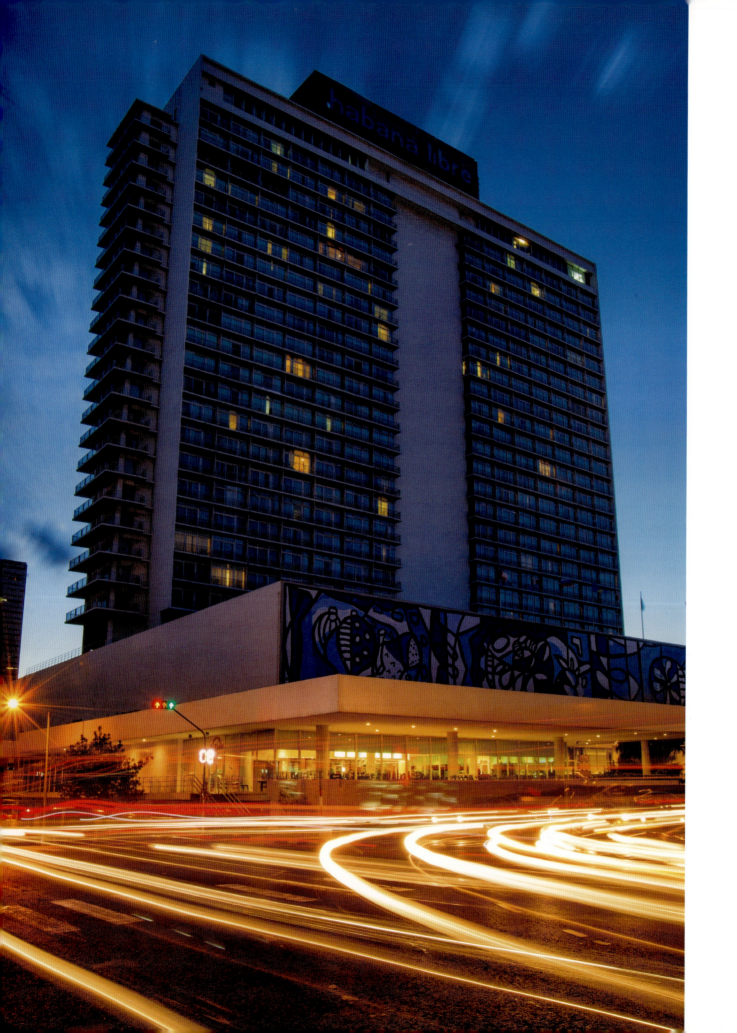

LEFT The twenty-seven story, 630-room Havana Hilton Hotel was designed by the Los Angeles firm Welton Becket & Associates and opened in 1958. It featured cantilevered balconies with steel balusters, interior shopping arcades, a rooftop bar and nightclub, a casino, and a swimming pool. It was Latin America's tallest and largest hotel. Less than a year later, Fidel Castro and his solders commandeered the hotel, took up residence, and made it their headquarters, renaming it Hotel Habana Libre (Hotel Free Havana).

ABOVE Detail of the hotel's massive tile wall mural was by Cuban artist Amelia Peláez, which appears over the entrance and was restored in 1997.

Havana's architects. In addition, the transition from eclecticism to rationalism had taken place, and this modern movement created a division between Cuban architects who firmly believed in the traditions and principles of the island's colonial architecture and those who just as firmly believed in more modernity in design. Each school of thought battled for ideological supremacy, while the common call for Cuban identity in the rationalist style continued to assert itself. Many of the theoretical debates, declarations, and doctrines were published in the architectural magazines of the day: *El Arquitecto, Colegio de Arquitectos de La Habana,* and *Arquitectura y Artes Decorativas.*

Beginning in the 1940s there was an assimilation of the repertory of forms of rationalism and notable architectural experiments in the regionalist aspect of rationalism, which was in accordance with Havana's tropical climate and the island's natural building materials. The Cuban neocolonial style (not to be confused with the modern regionalism or colonial revivalism of the 1950s) persisted into the late 1930s. The Albert Kaffenberg house, designed by Rafael de Cárdenas in 1938, may have been one of the last built in this style. The neocolonial is considered the last phase of the eclectic style in Cuba. Ironically, Cárdenas, a student of Leonardo Morales, was also one of the first Havana architects to, later, put the modernist style into practice.

⚜ ⚜ ⚜

ABOVE The Habana Libre lobby's canopy of circular skylights acts as a source of natural light. Integrating tropical foliage and light is characteristic of Cuban nationalist design.

RIGHT The famous ten-panel ceramic tile mural, *History of the Antilles* (1957) by Cuban artist René Portocarrero, is in the Habana Libre's Las Antillas Bar. The colorful mural depicts the Caribbean legend of the Antilles' women and flora.

LEFT The Habana Libre's interior design was assigned to James McQuaid, a member of Welton Becket's architectural firm. McQuaid saw that all materials in the hotel originated from Cuban manufacturers. This second-floor hallway is an example of modern design and Cuban elements.

RIGHT The hotel's lobby is a modernist architectural concept patterned after the traditional Cuban colonial palaces: an open inner courtyard with surrounding galleries, natural light, and vegetation.

ABOVE Originally the School of Domestic Sciences, this building was designed by José Pérez Benitoa in a stylized art deco fashion and built in 1940. It is now the San Alejandro School of Fine Arts, a high school specializing in the fine arts.

RIGHT A detail of a relief on the façade of the San Alejandro School.

ABOVE An Egyptian-style portico frames the entrance to the Havana-American Jockey Club of Cuba, designed in 1928 by the American firm Schultze and Weaver. The Jockey Club was next to Oriental Park Racetrack where thoroughbred horse racing was held during the winter months.

RIGHT Detail of the stained-glass Jockey Club entrance. Egyptian motifs were popular beginning in 1922, when Howard Carter astounded the world with his discovery of King Tut's tomb.

ABOVE Entrance to the Tropicana Cabaret Club designed by Max Borges Jr. The Tropicana is one of Cuba's most famous mid-century architectural gems.

World War II put an end to the art deco and streamline styles and their influence in Havana. A more studied mid-century modernism emerged, serving as a springboard to the International Style, whose name is attributed to the title of the catalogue to the groundbreaking 1932 exhibition at New York's Museum of Modern Art organized by architect Philip Johnson and architecture historian Henry-Russell Hitchcock. Characteristics common to the International Style were the rejection of ornament, simplification of form, and the adoption of steel, glass, and concrete as construction materials.

The end of World War II brought about a new era of sugar expansion that propelled Cuba's economic growth and another building boom. By the end of the 1940s Havana was once again, as in the early 1920s, enjoying prosperity. Wealth continued to accumulate and was manifested in the usual ways, the most obvious of which was the construction of modern buildings and lavish homes, this time in "country-club suburbia."

In proportion to Cuba's size and population, there was a very large number of professional architects working in Havana during the post–World War II years. Talents such as Nicolás Arroyo, Eugenio Batista, Alberto Beale, Max Borges Jr., Aquiles Capablanca, Rafael de Cárdenas, Manuel Copado, Mario Girona, Juan Ignacio Guerra, Manuel Gutiérrez, the firm of Junco, Gastón and Domínguez, Frank Martínez, Gabriela Menéndez, Ricardo Porro, Antonio Quintana, Nicolás Quintana, Mario Romañach, and Fernando Salinas played pivotal parts in modern architectural design in the complex and avant-garde theoretical context of universal and regional culture. A number of them explored and used Cuban colonial traditions in their residential works.

ABOVE Tropicana dancers perform for hundreds of patrons every night of the week. Artists such as Nat King Cole, Josephine Baker, Rita Montaner, and Carmen Miranda, performed there in the Club's early days.

Many architecture historians think of Eugenio Batista, considered to have been the foremost student of Leonardo Morales, as Cuba's most important early modernist and theoretician. An example of Batista's architectural theory can be seen in his notes for a lecture titled "Functions in Architecture," presented at the University of Oregon in 1966. Here is an excerpt:

> More than ever today, the field of architecture seems to be divided in two camps: those who, like Raphael, Peter Behrens and Mies van der Rohe are committed to reflection, serenity and order; and those who, together with Michaelangelo [sic], Gaudí and Frank Lloyd Wright prefer the exuberant expressions of excitement. Must we choose between these two attitudes, judging one to be correct and the other wrong? Is it possible to correlate the two? . . . Having completed our brief look, we can now try to decide how many things a building must do in order to deserve to wear the badge of "architecture." I suggest that we settle for three functions to be fulfilled, that I propose to call the physical, the intellectual, and the emotional functions of architecture. There is a fourth one, above all these: the spiritual function. Today we will leave this last one to the religious mystics and concentrate on the first three. . . . Integration, after all is said and done, remains the architect's chief responsibility.[19]

Batista's architecture synthesized colonial Cuban functionality of the past with a straightforward modernist aesthetic. He identified three architectural elements ("the three Ps")—patios, *portales* (porticoes), and *persianas* (louvers)—as essential to the renewal of Cuban traditions in the context of modern style. Havana's tropical climate was instrumental in the development of a variety of colonial sunscreening devices, from movable wooden jalousies,

LEFT Gambling in Cuba was prohibited after the 1959 revolution, and what was once the Tropicana's casino (managed by Lefty Clark) has been converted into a restaurant. The Tropicana still holds the reputation of the legendary nightclub that best symbolizes the glamour of pre-revolutionary Cuba.

ABOVE The indoor, air-conditioned Arcos de Cristal (Crystal Arches) Hall opened in 1951 and was designed with laminated thin-shell vaults and large expanses of glass, which allow views of the tropical foliage that was brilliantly lit during nighttime performances. The Crystal Arches Hall performances are scheduled during the very hot and/or rainy summer months.

RIGHT Never viewed by the public during daylight hours, Salón Bajo las Estrellas (Under the Stars Hall) has a seating capacity of more than a thousand and is surrounded by lush vegetation. Seen here are the Tropicana dancers practicing a new dance number; above the bandstand is architect Max Borges Jr.'s elliptical sculpture, which represents a mathematical formula in three dimensions.

stained glass, and fretted, openwork screens to permanent concrete brise-soleils. Other colonial elements such as the colorful glazed tiles known as azulejos were also incorporated into modern architecture.

Tourism in Cuba had begun in earnest during America's Prohibition in the 1920s and, after repeated slumps and heights, peaked with the Mafia-infested 1950s. By then Havana had become known as the "Paris of the Caribbean" and the grandest party city in the Americas. The city was rife with unbridled political corruption, gangsterism (*gangsterismo*), and daily strikes or protests, but all against the background of rising prosperity. Consequently, Havana's nightlife continued and was compared to Berlin's in the 1930s and Paris's in the 1920s. Because of gambling, the tropical atmosphere, and lively entertainment, the city was also considered the "Monte Carlo of the Americas" and became a destination stop for all the jet-setters of the day.

The notion of architectural tropicalization as it relates to tourism and modernism is a subject studied throughout the Caribbean islands, each of which has had its own individual approach. Architecture historians profess that because the Cuban government has discouraged tourism over the last fifty years, Havana's skyline has remained relatively unchanged since 1960, albeit with less polish than it had in its glory days.

By the 1950s the International Style had taken hold in Havana and the city's architecture was being well documented, as in New York's Museum of Modern Art's 1955 exhibition and publication titled *Latin American Architecture since 1945*.[20] America's foremost historian of modern architecture at the time, Henry-Russell

LEFT The 1920s *Fountain of the Eight Muses* by Italian sculptor Aldo Gamba was originally located outside the entrance of Havana's Gran Casino Nacional. In 1952 Martin Fox, owner of the Tropicana, purchased the fountain and had it installed outside his nightclub, best known through the 1950s for its roulette, rumba, and romance.

RIGHT *Ballerina*, a sculpture by Rita Longa at the entrance of Tropicana, has become the emblematic symbol of the club.

LEFT The María de los Dolores Puig house was designed by Mario Romañach and completed in 1955. Although modest in scale, it is typical Romañach in the use of bare bricks and a hidden side entrance. Most of Romañach's architecture has a maturity and confidence somewhat lacking in the work of his Cuban contemporaries.

ABOVE Mario Romañach was one of Cuba's most famous and talented modernists. This terrace, garden, and patio with decorative stained glass optimize continual air circulation to cool the house.

Hitchcock, introduced four of Havana's avant-garde modernists to an international audience: Max Borges Jr., Aquiles Capablanca, Gustavo Moreno, and Antonio Quintana, who among other notable Cuban architects of the 1940s and 1950s remain legendary throughout the Caribbean, Latin America, and the U.S. The MoMA exhibition led the way to a greater understanding of mid-twentieth-century Cuban architecture, especially within its social, political, and economic contexts.

Havana's landscape was changing fast. Many nineteenth- and early twentieth-century houses in Vedado were being torn down and replaced by skyscrapers in the International Style. The modernist structures ranged from apartment houses like FOCSA (acronym for Fomento de Obras y Construcciones, S.A.), built for an affluent clientele, to the tourist hotels Nacional, Hilton, and Riviera, to civic and private buildings like the Teatro Nacional and Cine Yara.

Havana was but one of the first Latin American cities to adopt modernism in residential architecture. Among the architects who participated in this building frenzy was Mario Romañach, who was described in *Havana: Districts of Light:*

> In the 1950s, the architects who were designing the great complexes of La Rampa at El Vedado and the modern homes of Nuevo Vedado were also building huge villas in bold modern designs in Cubanacán, where space was unlimited. The latter district contains some of the best work of the leading architects of the decade, in particular Mario Romañach. Romañach designed seventy buildings in a mere fifteen years (he left Cuba in 1960).[21]

Other examples of the International Style built during this golden age of Cuban architecture are found throughout the city.

ABOVE/LEFT The open dining room is filled with furniture from the 1950s with the contemporary lighting being the only addition.

ABOVE/RIGHT The dining area adjoins the kitchen where, other than updated appliances, everything has been kept original.

RIGHT The living room's small windows allow sufficient natural light and breezes to flow through the house, keeping the house cool from the tropical sun.

LEFT The current owners of this Romañach house spent years restoring it to the architect's original intent, including hand-scraping layers of paint off the bricks. The entrance displays the original elaborate brickwork and exotic wood carpentry.

One of the most renowned is the house the American architect Richard Neutra designed for Swiss banker Alfred von Schulthess in 1956. The main construction materials were tropical hardwoods, glass, and reinforced concrete. The tropical gardens surrounding the house were designed by Brazilian landscaper Roberto Burle Marx and are meant to integrate with the dwelling. Neutra's large plate-glass surfaces allow the home's interior and landscaped exterior to connect and convey a sense of being one with nature. The use of native materials, including West Indies mahogany (*Swietenia mahagoni*) and Cuban stone, helped humanize Neutra's International Style concept.

The Cuban revolution took place in 1959; not long after that, the U.S. established a trade embargo against Cuba in the 1960s—a key factor that forced architects and builders who remained on the island to find new formulas for construction, building materials, and methods that had been employed before the 1959 revolution.

The compelling history of the founding of the schools is best described in John Loomis's *Revolution of Forms: Cuba's Forgotten Art Schools*. Thus was the concept hatched:

> One late afternoon in January 1961, an unlikely pair of golfers, Fidel Castro and Che Guevara, enjoyed a few rounds on the well-manicured course of what had been the exclusive country club of Havana's elite. There they pondered the future of this unique site for a new society, in which exclusive country clubs would have no place. The beautifully landscaped country club was the crown jewel in Havana's most affluent suburb, aptly named Country Club Park.[22]

ABOVE Architect Miguel Gastón, famous for his collaboration in designing the Radiocentro complex in 1947, built this house overlooking the ocean in Miramar in 1952 for himself.

RIGHT Built on Le Corbusier–style *pilotis*, the elevated second floor contains all the main rooms, leaving the ground floor available for an open porch, carport, and saltwater swimming pool—a design that proves advantageous during hurricane season because of flooding.

ABOVE A view through the ground floor; the stairs to the upper floor are enclosed by the reflective glass wall and the pool on the ocean side.

THE NATIONAL SCHOOLS OF ART

At Fidel Castro's behest, Ricardo Porro was asked to put together a team to design and build what was to become Havana's National Schools of Art. Porro immediately hired two colleagues with whom he had previously worked in Venezuela to collaborate on the project: Italian architects Roberto Gottardi, who continues to reside in Havana, and Vittorio Garatti, who currently lives in Milan.

Soon thereafter the Havana Country Club was nationalized and Country Club Park was redubbed Cubanacán, after the island's indigenous name. The five schools were to be built on direct orders from Castro, who said in 1961, before ground was broken and architectural plans were developed, that the National Schools of Art were to be "the most beautiful academy of arts in the whole world," and lauded the architects as "artists."[23]

The designs of the five faculties of the academy were divided among the three idealistic young architects, and each school has its own autonomous space. Vittorio Garatti designed the School of Music and School of Ballet, Roberto Gottardi the School of Dramatic Arts, and Porro the School of Fine Arts and School of Modern Dance. While the five schools have aesthetic similarities, both Gottardi and Garatti incorporated an Italian neorealism, a kind of hybrid of academicism and modernism, in their buildings. All were constructed in economical local materials, including Cuban bricks, and feature Catalan vaults.

Gottardi, Venetian by birth, a stage designer, and student of the Italian neorationalist architect Franco Albini, achieved in his School of Dramatic Arts a contemporary interpretation of a fortress-like medieval Venetian city. The high brick walls enclose passageways and irregular spaces that seem to be sections of a

ABOVE The infinity saltwater swimming pool gives the illusion of floating into the sea and is often splashed with ocean waves on windy days.

maze. The narrow halls and compact volumetric areas lead to classrooms and internal courtyards that can easily remind one of Cuba's Spanish colonial traditions.

Garatti's School of Music consists of a series of half-buried structures that resemble a serpent twisting along the lush tropical topography of the Quibu River. The serpentine scheme of structures contains classrooms and individual practice rooms.

The brick galleries of Garatti's School of Ballet flow freely and follow the natural contour of the landscape, lending a feeling of integration with nature. The massive brick vaults and majestic brick dome of the recital hall denote a monumentality of performance by both the architect and the intended students. Unfortunately, when the school was nearly completed, Cuban prima ballerina Alicia Alonso, cofounder and director of the National Ballet of Cuba (with whom Garatti had worked closely on the design concept), refused to move her company to the site. Today it is completely abandoned and left to virtual ruins. In the 1970s Garatti was arrested for espionage, imprisoned, and then expelled from Cuba.

Porro's expressionist design for the School of Fine Arts included painting, printmaking, and sculpture studios; classrooms for academic studies; a foundry; and an exhibition hall, library, café, and administration offices. During my personal interviews with him in Paris, Porro explained that he envisioned the buildings to be part of a city with streets and piazzas with perspectives that would constantly change. A narrow arcade leading to the central piazza prolongs the three descending arches of the entrance that serves as an invitation. The oval painting and sculpture studios are covered by vaults with skylights and windows all around. They receive a maximum of natural light that allows the study from all angles of a model placed at the center. The exterior form of the studios can be seen as

LEFT The house of Timothy James Ennis was designed by Ricardo Porro and built in 1957; it displays a strong Le Corbusier influence and is the last private residence Porro built in Cuba.

ABOVE A predecessor to Porro's School of Fine Arts and Modern Dance, the Ennis house is an example of organic expressionism that follows the styles of modernism and postmodernism, especially in the handling of surfaces and space.

OVERLEAF Porro defines his architecture as "the creation of a poetic framework for the actions of man." The poetry of Porro's architecture is evident in both the curvilinear and the geometric lines and planes. His reference to a stylized representation of both male and female sexuality is seen here in the form of a gargoyle.

ABOVE The interior of the house is furnished with period furniture and Cuban contemporary art.

female breasts and the fountain in the central piazza as a papaya, a tropical fruit whose name is often used in Cuban parlance to refer to a woman's genitals. Porro further explained that his designs for the art school symbolize "Ochún, Eros, and Woman." He pointed out that Cuba is the only country of the African diaspora to have preserved the *babalaos*, or high priests of prophecy, who operate through the religion of Santeria (Rule of Ocha). He continued to say that with his School of Fine Arts he decided to express this tradition of black Cubans, an essential element of Cuban culture that had never before been reflected in the island's architecture. "I conceived it as an image of Ochún, African goddess of fertility, an important deity in all ancient civilizations."[24] (Porro wasn't the only one exploring the island's national identity and African heritage in his work; during the 1930s, 1940s, and 1950s other Cuban artists were depicting themes of the essence of *Cubanidad* in their art. Among them Amelia Peláez and Wifredo Lam immediately come to mind.)

Porro developed the buildings for his School of Modern Dance jointly with those for the School of Fine Arts, since both faculties are on the same site. Like the art school, the modern dance school was designed as a city with streets, piazzas, and arcades. It includes four large dance studios with dressing rooms, a small theatre for choreography, classrooms for academic studies, a library, café, and offices. The forms of the dance studios reflect a dancer's postures and gestures and express as well an important moment in history, that is, the idealistic first years of the Cuban revolution. "It was here," Porro said, "that I wanted to express two very intense feelings produced by this first, romantic stage of the Cuban revolution: elation and exaltation and its emotional explosion on the one hand, and anxiety and its uncertainty on the other. The result was

ABOVE This living area adjoins the dining room and follows the same interior-design scheme of period furniture mixed with Cuban contemporary art.

a constant mental strain of tension between conflicting emotions, a kind of agony, an agony in the etymological Greek meaning: that of struggle and combat."

The dance studios are covered by fragmented vaults to look as if they are sails inflated by expanding space. From above, the white walls, which serve as a background for the dancers and the receding trellised walls, reinforce this impression. As Porro pointed out, "The fragmented form of the fountain and the base of the columns pointing in different directions induce an uneasy feeling, as if we feared an unknown danger. Seen from above, the buildings look as if they are a glass shattered by a fist."[25]

The influence of International Style modernism in Porro's buildings is immediately recognizable as the integration of space with the surrounding landscape and the spatial definition achieved without formal enclosure. What Ricardo Porro accomplished with the schools is that he used his plan as an architectural analogy of the social and political freedom and openness to which the revolution aspired during its first romantic period, when as Porro explained "anything and everything was possible." Eduardo Luis Rodríguez, one of Cuba's foremost authorities on twentieth-century architecture, put it succinctly when he said, as quoted in Paul Goldberger's book *Building Up and Tearing Down*, "Porro wanted to make a statement about disorder against order, tranquility against tension. This complex started as a symbol of what the revolution could do in architecture, and then it became the opposite—a symbol of what the revolution didn't want."[26]

Havana's five National Schools of Art are touted by many young Cubans as the "only true example of Cuban revolutionary architecture" and by others as "unremarkable" and even "counterrevolutionary." Books and articles have been written about them, a very

LEFT Porro's early residential work evolved into an organic and personal expression of form, one that emphasized his avant-garde vision.

RIGHT The present owners of the house strive to keep the 1950s period look by decorating the interiors with furnishings from the mid-century era.

OVERLEAF The three-vault entrance to Porro's School of Fine Arts built in the former Country Club Park (now Cubanacán district) section of Havana.

ABOVE Porro's designs include Catalonian vaults constructed of locally made bricks to avoid the use of reinforced concrete.

RIGHT The central entry vault colonnade is part of the evocative School of Fine Arts design, conceived immediately after the revolution at a time of optimism and enthusiasm, "when everything still seemed possible," said Porro.

LEFT An interior view of one of the painting, studios with student Miguel Machado completing a series of his works.

ABOVE Both the controversial fountain in the shape of a papaya in the foreground and one of the painting studio pavilions with a glass cupola are references to the female body.

successful documentary film (*Unfinished Spaces*) has been released worldwide, and an opera on the subject is currently being composed. The schools are often described as distinguished, unorthodox, expressionist, neorealist, romantic modernist, and more, as James Lynch points out: "Labeled Baroque, even Mannerist, the National Schools of the Arts exalt an irrational, sensuous, undisciplined spirit profoundly disturbing to their critics. Space and form are mischievously, perhaps maliciously, warped, violated, and subjected to numerous visual and psychic shocks."[27] In the end, though, the majority of architecture historians and critics agree that Porro's, Gottardi's, and Garatti's designs and buildings reach a unique artistic level of true poetic expression rarely seen in the Western Hemisphere, and the schools as a whole are generally considered a masterwork.

Soon after the abandonment of the National Schools of Art and the closing of the College of Architectures, the Soviet Union was invited to establish a presence in Cuba. Architecture then became more of an instrument of political expression and began to exclusively serve the ideologies and sociopolitical reforms of a different revolutionary government. Development was restricted to Soviet-style housing and precepts.

PREVIOUS Porro's School of Modern Dance was designed with the movements of the dancer in mind.

ABOVE Vittorio Garatti's School of Ballet included three dance class pavilions, classrooms, a library, and an administration facility. The Royal Ballet of London's Carlos Acosta, who is Cuban, is working with British architect Norman Foster on a feasibility study to revive interest in restoring the ballet school.

RIGHT Practicing in Porro's School of Modern Dance are Angel, César, and Marcos Ramírez, twelve-year-old identical triplets who are members of Cuba's world-renowned National Ballet School and are featured in the 2014 award-winning documentary film, *To Dance Like a Man*.

OVERLEAF Today both Garatti's School of Ballet and Roberto Gottardi's School of Dramatic Arts are completely abandoned and in ruins, surrounded and engulfed by tropical jungle. Thankfully, UNESCO has added the schools to their "Tentative List of World Heritage Sites" and there is hope that these precious and important examples of Cuban expressionistic architecture will be restored and preserved.

ABOVE The Cubans much-loved Coppelia Ice Cream Parlor designed by Mario Girona and built in 1966 on the Vedado neighborhood's 23rd Street (Calle 23), better known as La Rampa. The flying saucer–shaped building and the gardens occupy an entire city block.

RIGHT Girona's biomorphic modernist architecture has stairs leading to the second floor, where different informal seating sections and lounges are available for patrons.

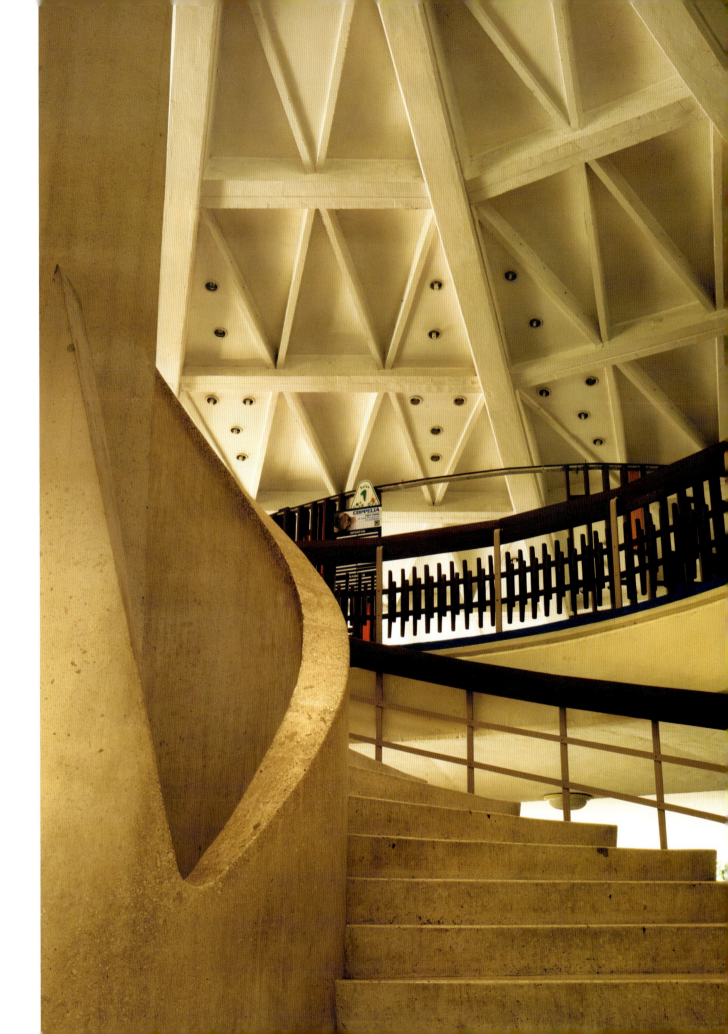

ABOVE An original interior colored-glass screen in the second-floor circular pavilion. All the original architectural elements and fixtures in Coppelia have been preserved.

CONCLUSION

UNESCO designated Havana a World Heritage Site in 1982. In recent years Eusebio Leal Spengler, Historian of the City of Havana and director of the restoration program of Old Havana, has overseen significant architectural rescue and preservation projects in that particular district. But it should not go unmentioned that with few exceptions the restoration, conservation, and preservation of twentieth-century architecture in Havana have mostly been ignored. Various architecture historians and scholars argue that because of the last fifty-five years of Cuba's political history the island has suffered from a lack of infrastructural improvement and growth. They go on to point out that many iconic modernist buildings are being lost due to deterioration or poorly thought-out modifications, and to a degree this is true. But in the same breath it can be rightly said that because of that political history and what I describe as "preservation by neglect," much of Havana's significant and important architecture, both domestic and civic, has been saved from destruction or disfigurement by insensitive profit-seeking development. This certainly includes Cuba's twentieth-century contributions to modern architecture. Although mid-century modern structures do not have the same protection designation as Havana's colonial buildings, many areas in the city's swank neighborhoods boast art deco, modern movement, and International Style mansions that are being cared for; once the houses of bankers and sugar industry magnates, they have become mostly embassies, "protocol" houses for dignitaries, and residences for government officials. The Cuban chapter of the international organization knows as Docomomo (Documentation and Conservation of Buildings, Sites and Neighborhoods of the Modern Movement), in addition to architects, scholars, and historians like Eduardo Luis Rodríguez, José Antonio Choy, and Mario Coyula, continually crusade to save twentieth-century modern

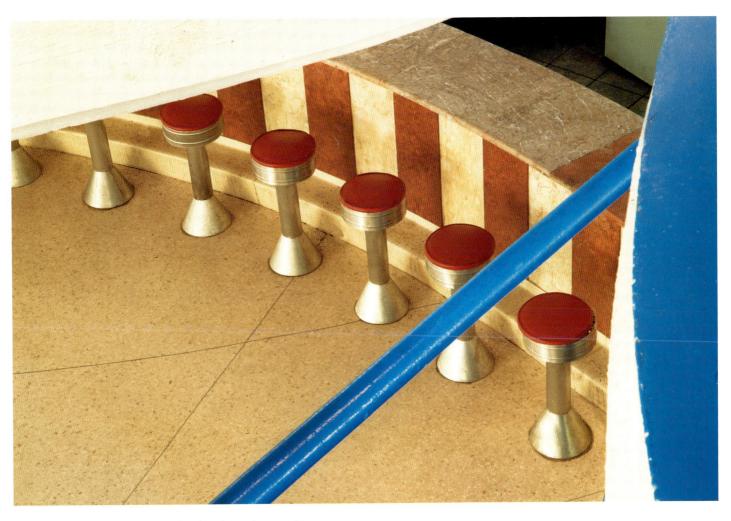

ABOVE Coppelia's counter, where nothing has changed since 1966, except the flavors of ice cream.

movement structures and envision a Havana preservation district in La Rampa area of Havana's Vedado neighborhood. It is long overdue that these once obscure twentieth-century architectural gems be lifted out of silence.

After traveling throughout Cuba for the last fifteen years, I've not only learned that mid-twentieth-century Cuban architects have never been fully appreciated and that their contributions warrant further research, I've also recognized how Cuba's socialist government, in favor of what it considers a more pragmatic construction ideal, has since the 1960s downgraded the practice of architecture and the role of the architect.

More recently, however, I have become more optimistic and now believe that Cuban architects and their unique aesthetics have a brighter future. As the Cuban government becomes less restrictive of its citizens' traveling off the island and loosens censorship of the Internet, island architects will become more aware of the latest global influences and opportunities for their talents and expertise.

Most Cuban historians, conservators, preservationists, and architects not only recognize the need to honor Cuba's modern movement buildings for their historically significant patrimony, but also have the desire to apply Cuba's unique architectural design traditions to twenty-first-century projects. The decades of censorship and restrictions on travel have served as incentives for Cuban architects to look beyond their own country in seeking the exchange of ideas that would allow them to design and produce works not just in Cuba but in the global environment as well. As Ricardo Porro explains, "Architecture must be more than a craft, it must be an art, and only an artist can make great architecture." Now is the time for Cuba to offer its architects and architecture students the best possible opportunities for sharing Cuban architectural traditions and aesthetics with a contemporary worldwide audience.

PREVIOUS A continually operating 1950s Havana service station. It is not accidental that the majority of the cars being serviced are also from the 1950s.

LEFT Nicolás Quintana's last architectural project in Cuba was the Banco Nacional de Cuba (National Bank of Cuba) in 1959 for then-Minister of Finance Ernesto (Che) Guevara. Construction was halted when Quintana went into exile, but work resumed in the 1970s and the building became the Hermanos Amejeiras hospital, which opened in 1982. The architecture illustrates the rationalist stage that had developed in Havana by the late 1950s.

ABOVE The access routes and interiors of the building were updated during its 1970s restoration, renovation, and renewal.

OVERLEAF The house of Alfred de Schulthess was designed by Richard Neutra, who was considered one of the masters of modern architecture, in collaboration with the Cuban firm Alvarez y Gutiérrez. It was built in 1958 in Havana's Cubanacán district, originally called Country Club Park, the city's equivalent of Beverly Hills.

LEFT Brazilian landscape architect Roberto Burle Marx designed the gardens that are, to this day, considered some of the finest in Cuba.

ABOVE The covered walkway from the driveway to the front door is supported by Neutra's trademark "spider-leg" colonnade and provides shelter from both the tropical sun and rain.

ABOVE A view of the dining room, where a paneled wall conceals pocket sliding doors that provide additional privacy.

RIGHT The entrance hall shows the rationalist concrete-and-glass design that emphasizes clarity of form and function and reflectes Neutra's championing of open-air living.

LEFT Neutra's de Schulthess residence is one of Havana's intact examples of important early modernist architecture. It was awarded the Gold Medal of the Cuban National Association of Architects in 1958.

RIGHT The indoor-outdoor living concept is continued throughout the house, which is filled with mid-century furnishings.

ABOVE The Rosita Hornedo Building was a residential hotel with 172 apartments, designed by Cristóbal Martínez Márquez and completed in 1956. Built by unsavory politician Alfred Hornedo and named after his second wife, Rosita, it is situated in Havana's La Puntilla area where the Almendares River meets the sea. Hornedo and his wife occupied the triplex penthouse.

RIGHT The four-story La Puntilla commercial center in Havana's Miramar district was designed by José Antonio Choy and Julia Léon. Completed in 2001, the postmodernist design explores the use of primary colors and massive geometric forms. La Puntilla has become a major shopping center with boutiques, restaurants, an ice-cream parlor, and different kinds of shops.

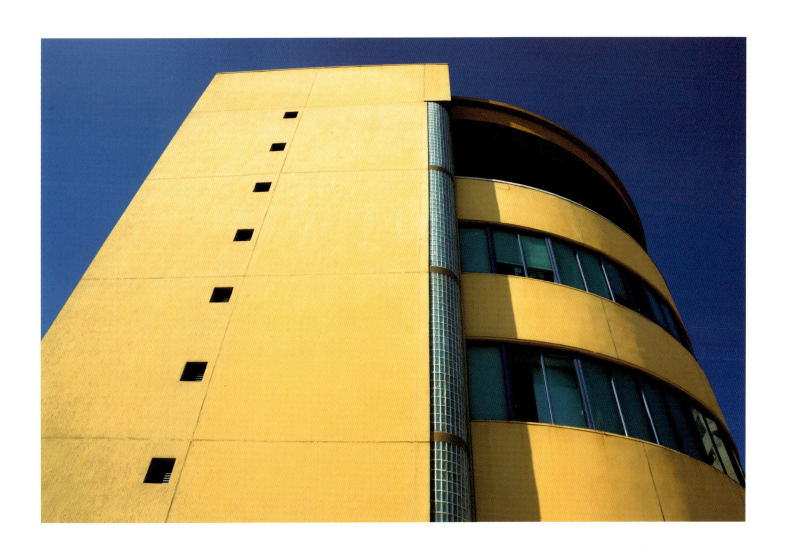

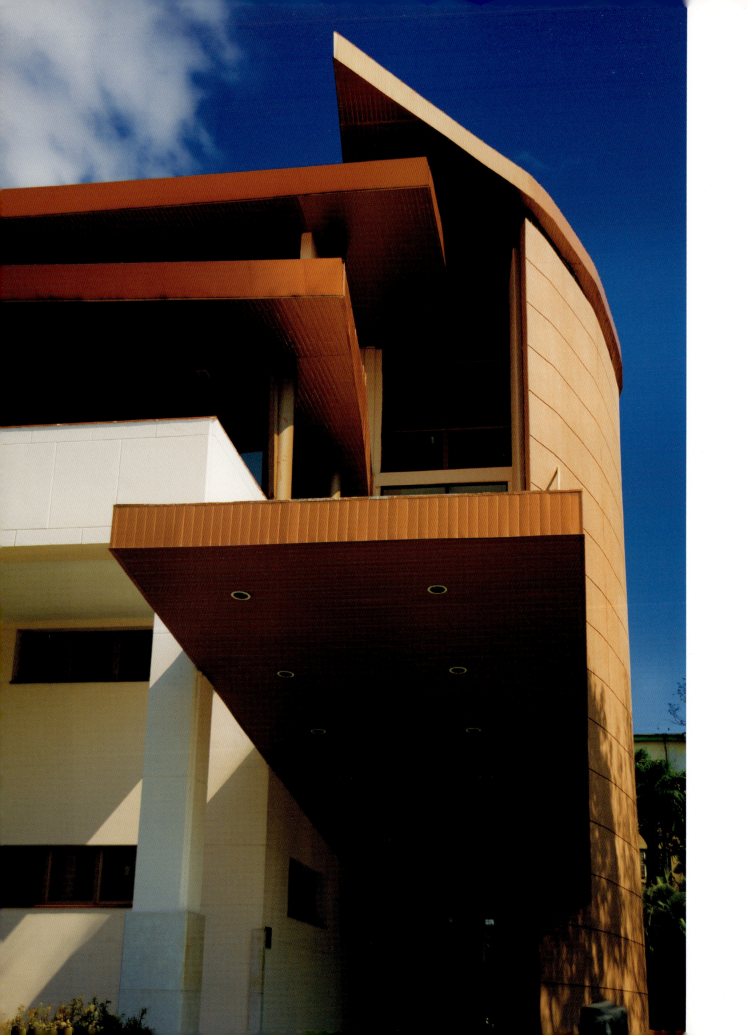

LEFT Entrance to what was originally the Trust Company of Cuba Bank, designed by Eugenio Batista in 1957. Cuban architects José Antonio Choy and Julia Léon, while respecting the integrity of Batista's original design, enhanced and expanded the bank in 1997, which is today named Banco Financiero Internacional.

ABOVE Palacio de Las Convenciones (International Convention Center) was inaugurated in 1979 and is thought to be one of the few successful attempts at postmodernism architecture after the 1959 revolution. Designed by Antonio Quintana, the building has broad bands of windows and incorporates open courtyard-like lobbies with fountains and tiled floors.

ACKNOWLEDGMENTS

As with any book such as this there are countless people to thank and acknowledge. The person I would like to begin with is my late friend Juan Carlos Granados. Juan was a simple but learned person. He sold books and antique magazines from a bookstall on Plaza de Armas in Old Havana. Over the past ten years we became friends while we discussed Cuban architecture, the island's colonial era and, more recently twentieth-century interiors. I practiced my deficient Spanish and Juan practiced his broken English. One of the amazing things about Juan Carlos was that he could find any reference book or antique magazine I required for my research. Sadly, he died in 2013 and I'll never be able to thank him again for his friendship or let him know how his valuable assistance helped facilitate my research and writing over the years. Juan Carlos symbolized what I value most about Cuba: its people. In every Cuban architectural tour I've led, lecture and presentation I've delivered in the U.S., or conversation I've had about Cuba, I'm asked what I like most about the island. My immediate answer is the Cuban people. They are welcoming, devoted, resourceful, industrious, generous, and sincere. For this reason, part of me will always feel that Cuba is a second home. Thank you, Juan Carlos.

I am forever grateful to María de Lourdes (Luly) Duke, founder and president of Fundación Amistad. Luly opened doors in Cuba for my photographer and me and facilitated the agenda and resources that made this book possible. As a board member for more than a decade at Fundación Amistad, a nonprofit foundation dedicated to cultural and education exchange with Cuba, it has been my pleasure to expand and refine my academic understanding of Cuba's unique five-hundred-year history in architecture and the decorative arts and to lead Fundación Amistad tours focusing on these aspects of its culture. I am also grateful to Fundación Amistad's staff, Celene Almagro, Martha Castellanos and Natalia Saavedra, for their assistance in organizing my visits to Cuba. Their help with the logistical arrangements, and their continual follow-up, helped to make every visit successful.

A few years ago I was fortunate enough to meet the exceptionally talented Cuban fine art photographer Nestor Martí, who lives in Havana. Nestor and I became friends and decided to work on this book together. His work with me centered on the intersection of twentieth-century Cuban history and culture as manifested through architecture and interiors. My sincere thanks goes out to Nestor for giving the 200 percent it takes to produce the work we've accomplished. I would also like to thank the other photographers who contributed: Paolo Gasparini, Brent Winebrenner, Jorge Alberto Laserna, Vanessa Rogers, Jorge García, Liz Netto, and the architect Kiovet Sánchez Alvarez.

I am indebted to Mónica Fernández, the cultural manager and researcher at Havana's Center for Modern Architecture, Urban Planning and Design. As a translator and academic liaison, her contributions of scholarly research lead to a partnership that I will forever value and I look forward to working with her on my next book that features Cuba.

This book had a most auspicious beginning with my introduction in Paris to Cuban architect Ricardo Porro and his wife Elena. My discussions with Mr. Porro led me to meet many other important Cuban architects to whom I owe a debt of gratitude.

I especially want to thank José Antonio Choy, his wife, Julia León, and their daughters, Adriana and Olivia Choy, all part of the Choy-León Architecture Studio in Havana. I appreciate the time architect and artist Juan Luis Morales gave me during our conversations in his Paris studio. Special thanks also to Mario Coyula, Isabel Rigol, Miguel Coyula, Jose Fornés, Renán Rodríguez, and Renaud de La Noue. I want to acknowledge architects Roberto Gottardi, his collaborator Carlos Rodríquez, and Vittorio Garatti for their contributions, and also Eduardo Luis Rodríguez for his invaluable works on the subject of twentieth-century Cuban architecture.

This is my fourth book that features Cuban architectural and material culture and I extend my thanks to all the Cuban historians, preservationists, and officials who guided me through the politics of gaining permissions.

I've had the good fortune to have received advice from Eusebio Leal, Havana City Historian; Gladys Collazo, President of the Cuban Heritage Committee; Patricia Rodríguez, Director of Havana's Master Plan; Sonia Ortega, Vice Dean of International Relationships at National Art School, and Yasim Herrera, Sub-Director of Artistic and Pedagogic at the same school; Alfredo Ruiz, Director of International Relations of the Ministry of Culture and Vice President of Casa de las Américas Marcia Leiseca; Katia Varela and Gustavo González, Director and Vice Director of the Decorative Arts Museum; Irina Carulla, Casa de la Amistad Public Relations; Gloria Alvarez, Director of the Historical Photograph Library at the Havana City Historian's Office;

ENDNOTES

and Moraima Clavijo, Director of the National Art Museum. From the Havana UNESCO office I am grateful to director Herman van Hooff and UNESCO officer Victor Marín. Without their intercession I would not have been able to visit many of the Havana locations. I also want to thank Argel Calcines, editor of *Opus Habana* magazine for his encouragement and support over the years; Reny Martínez for all his location suggestions and introductions to Cubans in the arts; Rena Pérez-Grossman for answering the hard questions; Remberto Ramírez for many memorable Cuban dinners; Alysa Nahmias for her film *Unfinished Spaces* and the additional insight on Cuba's National Schools of Art; and artist Miguel Machado.

I would also like to mention Michael Parmly, the former United States Chief of Mission at the U.S. Interests Section in Havana and his wife Marie-Catherine for their hospitality at the United States Ambassador's residence; Ambassador Peter Burkhard of Switzerland; Ambassador Dianna Melrose of Great Britain; Director of Fototeca de Cuba Nelson Ramírez; Jossie Alonso; and Ahnedel Machado Pérez (Titi).

My appreciation goes to Karolina Stefanski for her methodical research and organizational skills and the endless transcribing she contributed.

Lastly, I'd like to thank my editor Ellen Cohen who has patiently and expertly guided me through my last four books; her extreme professionalism and understanding has no limits. My gratitude to Charles Miers, Rizzoli's publisher for recognizing the importance and historical significance of twentieth-century Cuban architecture and the vision to allow me to present it to the public. Also thanks to the talented and creative designer Federico Pérez Villoro of MGMT. design for his inventiveness and imagination in designing this book.

Finally, I want to sincerely thank and acknowledge *los habaneros* (the people of Havana) and the Havana homeowners who invited me into and allowed me to photograph their homes so that I could show the world that the vibrant style and spirit for which Cuba is known remains a strong part of its culture.

1. Hugh Thomas, *Cuba, or, The Pursuit of Freedom* (New York: Da Capo Press, 1971, 1998), 497.
2. Ibid., 498.
3. Leonardo Morales y Pedroso, "La arquitectura en Cuba de 1898 a 1929," trans. Mónica Fernández, *El Arquitecto* 4, no. 38 (May 1929): 433.
4. María Luisa Lobo Montalvo, *Havana: History and Architecture of a Romantic City* (New York: Monacelli Press, 2000), 263.
5. Ricardo Porro, "Villa Villegas, La Havane," *L'architecture d'aujourd'hui*, no. 350 (Jan.–Feb. 2004), 71.
6. James Anthony Froude, *The English in the West Indies* (London: Longmans, Green, and Co., 1888), 293.
7. Joseph L. Scarpaci, Roberto Segre, and Mario Coyula, *Havana: Two Faces of the Antillean Metropolis*, rev. ed. (Chapel Hill: University of North Carolina Press, 2002), 52.
8. Cathryn Griffith, *Havana Revisited: An Architectural Heritage* (New York: W. W. Norton & Company, 2010), 121.
9. John Paul Rathbone, *The Sugar King of Havana: The Rise and Fall of Julio Lobo, Cuba's Last Tycoon* (New York: Penguin Books, 2010), 75.
10. Scarpaci, Segre, and Coyula, *Havana: Two Faces*, 57.
11. Thomas, *Cuba, or, The Pursuit of Freedom*, 540.
12. Alejo Carpentier, *La ciudad de las columnas* (Havana: Editorial Letras Cubanas, 1982), 13, 14.
13. Richard Gott, *Cuba: A New History* (New Haven: Yale University Press, 2004), 129.
14. José Cantón Navarro, *History of Cuba: The Challenge of the Yoke and the Star* (Havana: Si-Mar S.A., 2001), 89.
15. María Luisa Lobo Montalvo and Zoila Lapique Becali, "The Years of Social," *Journal of Decorative and Propaganda Arts* 22, Cuba theme issue (1996): 105.
16. Ibid., 112.
17. Louis A. Pérez Jr., *On Becoming Cuban: Identity, Nationality, and Culture* (New York: Harper Collins, 1999), 281.
18. Jean-François Lejeune, "The City as Landscape: Jean Claude Nicolas Forestier and the Great Urban Works of Havana, 1925–1930," *Journal of Decorative and Propaganda Arts* 22, Cuba theme issue (1996): 165.
19. Eugenio Batista, notes for "Functions in Architecture" (lecture, University of Oregon, Eugene, March 8, 1966). Private papers of Eugenio Butista, Cuban Heritage Collection, University of Miami Libraries, Coral Gables, FL.
20. Henry-Russell Hitchcock, *Latin American Architecture since 1945* (New York: Museum of Modern Art, 1955).
21. Juan Luis Morales Menocal and Xavier Galmiche, *Havana: Districts of Light* (Paris: Vilo International, 2001), 162
22. John A. Loomis, *Revolution of Forms: Cuba's Forgotten Art Schools*, updated ed. (New York: Princeton Architectural Press, 2011), 19.
23. Morales Menocal and Galmiche, *Havana: Districts of Light*, 162.
24. Ricardo Porro, in interviews by the author, December 2010–October 2013.
25. Ibid.
26. Paul Goldberger, *Building Up and Tearing Down: Reflections on the Age of Architecture* (New York: Monacelli Press, 2009), 57.
27. James Lynch, "Cuban Architecture since the Revolution," *Art Journal* 39, no. 2 (Winter 1979–80): 101.

First published in the United States of America in 2014 by

Rizzoli International Publications, Inc.
300 Park Avenue South
New York, NY 10010
www.rizzoliusa.com

Designed by MGMT. design

Rizzoli Editor: Ellen R. Cohen

ISBN: 978-0-8478-4346-6
Library of Congress Control Number: 2014939173

Copyright © 2014 Michael Connors

All rights reserved. No part of this publication may be reproduced, stored in a retrieval system, or transmitted in any form or by any means, electronic, mechanical, photocopying, recording, or otherwise, without prior consent of the publisher.

Printed in China

2014 2015 2016 2017 2018 / 10 9 8 7 6 5 4 3 2 1

Photo Credits (Numbers refer to page numbers)

All photography by Néstor Martí except for the following:

Kiovet Sánchez Alvarez: 136, 137
Jorge García: 61
Paolo Gasparini: 14, 19
Jorge Alberto Laserna: 232, 233
Liz Netto: 234, 235, 237, 238, 239
Vanessa Rogers: 20, 21
Brent Winebrenner: 32, 33, 39, 40, 41, 42, 48, 49, 50, 53, 133, 162, 230, 231, 236, 240, 241

PAGES 246/247 The distinctive Max Borges Jr. design, based on lightweight concrete parabolic shells, covers the 1953 Club Náutico.

PAGES 248/249 View of Havana from the La Puntilla area across the Almendares River. In the distance is a pair of 1950s apartment skyscrapers in Vedado. After the revolution they became residence halls for medical students.

PAGES 250/251 The 1957 Riviera Hotel situated on the Malecón at sunset. Before the revolution Havana was considered one of the bastions of modern architecture and, because of "preservation by neglect," many important mid-century buildings still exist.

PAGES 252/253 Sunset on the Malecón, Havana's seaside boulevard promenade overlooking the Straits of Florida.